LITTLE BOOK OF
BRITISH STEAM

Charlie Morgan

LITTLE BOOK OF
BRITISH
STEAM

First published in the UK in 2008

© Demand Media Limited 2012

www.demand-media.co.uk

Printed and bound in China

ISBN 978-1-909217-20-1

Contents

Chapter 1

A History of Steam

FOR MORE THAN 100 YEARS, steam locomotives were the most technologically advanced form of power and transport dominating the railways and often described as the "heartbeat" of the UK. The earliest railways used horse-power to pull carts along the track, but the age of steam was just beginning to take shape and locomotives were in early development in the 1700s. By 1804, Richard Trevithick had created a locomotive that had mixed success and ran on a narrow gauge tramway in Wales, but the first locomotive to have more than a modicum of success was George Stephenson's Rocket in 1829.

Most railway locomotives were organised into classes with each class essentially having its own design and specific role. Most were also given a code which more often than not was based on the locomotive's wheel arrangement. Railways were designed as a confined track for locomotives to move heavy loads at relatively high speeds with the rail both supporting and guiding the vehicle. The development of the actual railway itself may even have been an accident.

Wheels often left tracks in dirt roads and the Greeks during the Age of Pericles made stone ways similar to tracks in order to transport heavy stone for theatre and monument building. Developments continued and crossed Europe to the UK where it was not unknown for certain regions to have wooden railways during the time of Elizabeth I. By the 1600s, wooden railways were fairly common and by the early 1700s – certainly in iron mining

areas – wooden tracks were replaced with iron ones. But the first railway that really took off in the UK was the Tanfield Wagon Way, a mining railway in County Durham. By 1727 it included Causey Arch, built by Ralph Wood, which was to become the railway's first viaduct.

The first public railway in the world was the Surrey Iron Railway at

ABOVE The steam engine designed and built by George Stephenson

RIGHT Engraving showing incomplete drawing of Richard Trevithick's steam locomotive

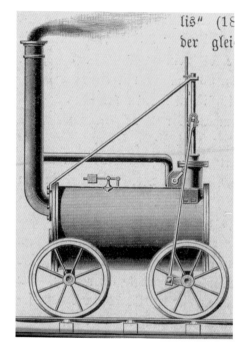

military and civil engineering, the locomotive had been invented and built. One of the pioneers of steam was Sir Isaac Newton who contributed to the idea of a kettle on wheels that could be propelled by its own steam. Then Frenchman, Nicolas Cugnot, produced a primitive tractor which could propel itself along by steam. Two Cornishmen, William Murdoch and Richard Trevithick, were to pioneer steam traction.

Several Trevithick locomotives were built, each a small, high-pressure stationary engine. One of these engines, Black Billy, was taken to Tyneside where a young Stephenson was to take a great deal of interest. While all this was taking place the first passenger line had already opened in South Wales in 1807. Horse-drawn carts with fare-paying passengers were a part of daily life on the Oystermouth Railway. Although not a commercial viability it seems incredible to think that eight years before the Battle of Waterloo, both steam traction and paying passengers on the railway were

Wandsworth which had up and down tracks allowing for two-way traffic. The railway was incorporated in 1803 and began at Wandsworth Wharf running through Croydon, Merstham and Godstone to the quarries at Coulsdon. Also at this time, despite the fact that mechanical engineering lagged behind

already quite well established.

In 1830, the Liverpool and Manchester Railway was the first railway to radically change both the commercial and social outlook of the industry with mechanical traction, up and down tracks, proper stations, timetables and primitive signalling. At first signalling took place with hand signals, then flags and lamps (complete with candles) at night. However, semaphore was adapted to visual railway signalling at the beginning of the 1840s. Semaphore rivalled for years with boards that were vertically pivoted and signalmen used red lamps at night for danger and white for clear. Interestingly, green lamps were used for "approach with caution", although obviously, this later changed to "clear" or "go". But travel by rail was relatively safe given that speeds were moderate, if not slow. However, the commercial success of the railways was anything but slow and the impact of the new phenomenon was huge. Quite simply, railways changed the world.

The railways generally followed old trade routes in the UK, as they did in the rest of Europe, linking cities, towns and industry. In parts of the US this same idea was followed, however, for many other places it opened up a whole new world and many of the American cities today were built by those pioneering the railways, including Atlanta, Atlantic City and Anchorage. The success of the Liverpool and Manchester line brought about the network of lines that all ran from London. These included lines to Birmingham, Southampton, Bristol,

BELOW A train passes under Rainhill Bridge on the Liverpool and Manchester Railway. Built in 1829, the bridge was the first to cross a railway at an angle

Manchester, Edinburgh and Glasgow. Entrepreneurs sprang up left, right and centre, ready to capitalise on the profits that the railways would bring. One such man was George Hudson from York who quickly recognised that his home town was a central point for railways in eastern England and the Midlands.

An unscrupulous man, Hudson's career was cut short when he became the focal point of an inquiry into the York and North Midland Railway – but a huge railway had already been built. In terms of building the railway networks it was a bit of a free for all and many disagreements and disputes broke out as companies and individuals either built parallel lines or fought over designated land. However, people's lives changed

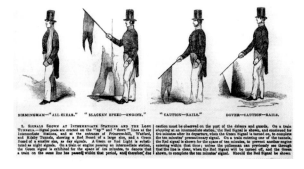

DIRMINGHAM—"ALL CLEAR."   "SLACKEN SPEED—ENGINE."   "CAUTION—RAILS."   DOVER—CAUTION—RAILS.

2. SIGNALS SHOWN AT INTERMEDIATE STATIONS AND THE LONG TUNNELS.—Signal posts are erected on the "up" and "down" lines at the Intermediate Stations, and at the entrance of Primrose-hill, Watford, and Kilsby Tunnels, showing a Red Board of a large size, and a Green Board of a smaller size, as day signals. A Green or Red Light is substituted as night signals. On a train or engine passing an intermediate station, the Green signal is exhibited for the space of ten minutes, to denote that a train on the same line has passed within that period, and therefore, due caution must be observed on the part of the drivers and guards. On a train stopping at an intermediate station, the Red Signal is shown, and continued for five minutes after its departure, when the Green Signal is turned on, to complete the ten minutes' precautionary signal. On a train entering one of the tunnels, the Red signal is shown for the space of ten minutes, to prevent another engine entering within that time; unless the policeman can previously see through that the line is clear, when the Red Signal will be turned off, and the Green shown, to complete the ten minutes' signal. Should the Red Signal be shown

forever and by the mid 1800s London was getting its beer from Burton on Trent, Yorkshire wool and coal were easily transported and fresh bread became part of daily life in the Scottish Highlands.

In the earliest locomotives of the Middleton Colliery, engines were driven by a cog-wheel to a single rack with two cylinders emerging from the centre-flue boiler. Then came Stephenson's second locomotive that had two axles that were independently driven, coupled by a pair of chains on sprockets with a central-flue boiler. His later engine, Locomotion, was the first to run on a steam public railway in 1925 on the Stockton and Darlington Railway. The Rocket was built by George Stephenson, Robert Stephenson and Henry Booth to enter a competition in 1829. Robert Stephenson, son of George, was the first engineer to become a millionaire. Also pioneering locomotives in 1829 was the Swedish-born John Ericsson who entered his own locomotive in the same competition. Novelty was a light motive unit where its only weak point was the boiler that lay on its side. The locomotive proved to be one of the four fastest steam engines, but would never make it commercially. By the end of the 1800s and the early 20th century, steam locomotives as built by the likes of Thomas Russell Crampton are more in line with those remembered today. These engines could speed along – as was proved by the City of Truro that was the first steam locomotive to exceed 100mph on 9 May 1904 – and were efficient and successful passenger trains.

Chapter 2

Underground Steam

IT IS PERHAPS DIFFICULT TO believe that traffic was so bad even then but underground steam began to take shape when the traffic problems in London were first highlighted more than a century ago. In the absence of a congestion charge – or indeed anything like it – moving around London from the West End to the City was a long drawn-out affair and hackney cabs and horse-drawn carriages fought their way past each other and the numerous carts that jammed the main streets. Policemen were positioned along notorious hot spots in the hope of easing the problem but this was not fail-safe and a plan was devised to take the successful steam railways underground.

Many thought the project was impossible but by the beginning of the 1860s the first section of the Metropolitan Railway was under construction following the line of the streets from Paddington to Farringdon. Sir John Fowler was the project engineer charged with making the plan viable and the most obvious problem he faced was the trapped steam underground. He needed a smokeless locomotive.

The resulting locomotive was nicknamed Fowler's Ghost and was a sturdy locomotive that produced no steam – however this resulted in not much power either. The locomotive had a small firebox with a long cylindrical chamber that was filled with fire bricks which were intended to be brought to a white heat and would then deputise for a real fire. The first underground line opened on 10 January 1863 and ran on broad gauge tracks maintained by the Great Western Railway. Daniel Gooch, a

pioneer of steam locomotives, designed and produced a set of tank engines with surface condensers which coped with the exhaust steam while the smoke trailed off behind in the tunnels. After each journey the boiling water was run off and cold water replaced it in time for the next trip. Carriages underground were lit by coal gas – a huge innovation at the time – which was transported in rubber bags enclosed in boxes on the roofs. GWR and the Metropolitan Railway fell out soon after the line opened and the underground company

Locomotives would have to vigorously exhaust after leaving the underground tunnels and water would be changed often to prevent too much smoke from filling the system. Obviously by today's standards conditions in the tunnels were frightening, but the trains were a success, passengers survived and commercially it was an extremely profitable venture. The underground slowly grew and it wasn't long before lines were extended and new routes were introduced.

had to employ the locomotives of Great Northern Railway for a time until it had built up sufficient locomotives of its own.

Locomotive manufacturer Beyer Peacock – builder of the U1 Garratt – produced a newly designed locomotive for the underground in 1864 which ran on standard gauge. These locomotives ran on both the Metropolitan and newly established District lines until the introduction of electrification in 1905.

Other underground railways began to appear with the first taking shape in Liverpool with the Mersey Railway passing under the river to Birkenhead in 1886 and the Glasgow City and District Railway the same year while the Glasgow Central underground line opened some 10 years later. While the UK large underground networks were beginning to appear, the US tried a different approach with overhead railways that although noisy were cheap to run and popular with ticket-buying customers. These were firmly established by the 1870s onwards – particularly in New York – although steam locomotives were gradually dying out in the cities worldwide by the early 20th century due to legislation banning smoke emissions in highly populated areas. However, these early beginnings have provided countless cities across the globe with a relatively cheap and often hassle-free way of travelling around some of the busier and densely populated areas.

BELOW The Great Northern, Piccadilly and Brompton underground tube route linking London stations, 1906

Chapter 3

The Image of Steam

WITH SO MUCH COMPETITION between rail companies before the 1923 grouping of the railways where more than 300 smaller companies were merged into just four, the image of each station, the buildings and staff were of paramount importance. Stations were where passengers were given their first impressions of the company that was about to transport them and station staff were the mainstay of the company. Working for the railways was more than just a job – it was a way of life. Stations were also designed to be more than just the bricks and mortar that sheltered passengers while they were waiting to travel. They had to be somewhere to book tickets, survey timetables and offer refreshments, and staff needed to be on hand to help with enquiries. Then there was the luggage – often heavy and bulky – that needed to be man-handled from taxis, the underground, buses and private vehicles to the steam locomotives themselves. Bookstalls and bars were a later addition to the stations. It was the station staff from the stationmaster down who made each railway company what it was.

The stationmaster was the most high-profile member of the railway companies' staff who needed a visible, hands-on approach. Most stationmasters had diverse responsibilities depending on the size of the station, the regularity of services and the volume of traffic – both trains and passengers – that passed through the station. Each and every passenger expected the stationmaster to know the answers to all their queries and expectations of the individual in charge were high. The smaller stations often dealt with a high volume of goods traffic and it was prudent for the stationmaster to be acquainted with the particular needs and demands of local businesses and traders.

The two key areas of responsibility for this pivotal figure were safety in train working and the security of buildings, equipment stores and money as well as the staff working under him. The stationmaster was also responsible for ensuring that trains were punctual, that they were clean, along with the station and that standards among the staff were high.

At the beginning of the 20th century more than 90% of signalmen and crossing keepers worked a 12-hour day and rarely had time off. In addition, holidays were short-lived often only lasting two or three days a year. Things were not much better for drivers and firemen who could work up to 15 hours a day with only the occasional Sunday off. Often platelayers and gangers fared better with shorter working days and most Sundays off – although there was always the possibility of problems on the line which would put paid to a well-earned rest.

Inspectors possibly had the easiest time with short working days (10 hours) and most weekends off. Despite the long hours, lack of holidays and relatively low pay – most railway employees earned less than £1.25 a week – the railways were viewed as a good employer who offered a "safe" job that could offer training and education to high standards for all employees who could then work their way up through the ranks. Railway employees took pride in doing a good job and the responsibility of the passengers was taken extremely seriously by all concerned.

BELOW Station masters were usually male but there were exceptions

Chapter 4

What Passengers Could Expect

DESPITE THE LAVISH STATIONS, expert staff and the all-knowing stationmaster, passengers were not always assured of a comfortable ride on the steam locomotives they travelled on. Railways were the first mode of transport to ferry passengers on long journeys relatively quickly although the notion that everyone could travel – even though it was offered – was not recognised by many.

Class mattered, just as it did throughout society at the time, and many trains only offered first and second class tickets which did not include those on lower incomes who required a lesser class of travel in order to afford it. However, even though the class system still applied,

it soon became possible for more people to travel during the late 19th century when a third class was introduced. But the classes, that were by now divided into upper, middle and lower, were not always a joyful experience as Victorian coaches usually meant a bumpy ride across the rail network. First class was often quite lavish while second class was much sparser. But, third class was a real test of endurance and passengers could often just hope to stay dry and pray that delays were short so that the ordeal couldn't get any worse.

With nationalisation still a long way off, conditions across the various railway companies varied with Great Western Railway and North Western and Midland Railway offering better conditions for third class passengers than most. It wasn't until basic facilities were introduced during the 1870s that conditions improved and London and North Western Railway were the first to introduce toilets in its sleeper cars. The first dining car was in place by the end of 1879 on the Great Northern Railway between London King's Cross and Leeds – although to make it more exclusive the entire carriage was separated from the remainder of the train. Midland Railway pioneered the plight of the third class passenger and announced that from 1872 all passengers would be eligible to travel on all its services. Midland then abolished middle class and reduced the cost of first class fares. The competition between rival companies then turned to providing facilities for passengers

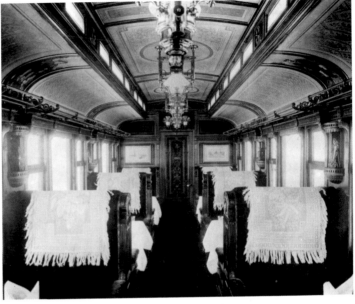

and not restricting them. GWR was the first company to introduce corridor trains in 1891. By the turn of the century competition was intense and the race to ensure the most luxurious surroundings for passengers with the most upgraded services was on. By the lead up to World War I passenger trains were elegant and business was booming.

ABOVE The elegant dining car on a Great Northern and MS & L train, 1888

Chapter 5

The Lines

GWR

FOUNDED IN 1833, GREAT WESTERN Railway (GWR), also known as "God's Wonderful Railway", was a feat of civil engineering connecting the West Country with South Wales and London. The line was not renowned for being direct in places and some fondly referred to it as the "Great Way Round". But despite the organisation of some of its early lines, GWR was known as the holiday railway – for taking vast numbers of British holidaymakers to the south west – and was largely built because of the demand from industries based in Bristol who wanted to maintain the city's prominence in the UK as a top trade connection to the US. This position was under some threat from other cities fast developing, including London, and because the River Avon – principally Bristol's link for imports and exports – was becoming clogged by silt, therefore making it more and more difficult to operate effectively as a major port.

Great Western Railway was founded two years prior to being incorporated by an Act of Parliament in 1835 and the legendary Isambard Kingdom Brunel, who became responsible for such incredible engineering such as the railway bridge over the River Tamar linking Plymouth in Devon with Saltash in Cornwall was appointed chief engineer. At the tender age of 27, Brunel himself undertook the surveying of the entire route between Bristol and London and made two major decisions along the way. First, he decided to route the line through the Marlborough Downs – with no major towns or cities – and second, he advocated that the line should be broad gauge, so as to allow larger wheels a smoother ride at higher speeds. The idea was to create a much more spectacular line here than was being devised and built to the north of London.

Daniel Gooch was appointed superintendent of locomotives and together the two men worked on the line – and its engines – with the first stretch of line opening between London and Taplow three years later. It took a further three years for the line between the capital and Bristol Temple Meads to be completed in 1841 when Box Tunnel was opened. The early locomotives used on the line were not particularly satisfactory, but with Gooch's involvement, the journey from Bristol to London proved to be a great success. Locomotive works were located in Swindon while the line continued to grow and bring continued prosperity to the people of Bristol. Over the next 22 years, lines were incorporated, amalgamated and built and many new companies were incorporated to run the new, improved or elongated railways including the Bristol and Exeter Railway, the Oxford and Rugby Railway, the South Wales Railway and the "holiday lines" including the Cornwall Railway, the South Devon Railway and the West Cornwall Railway. Due to the broad gauge lines of Brunel, passengers travelling on another line – the Birmingham and Gloucester Railway – were required to change trains at Gloucester which only operated on

Men at work in the Great Western Railway works in Swindon, 1875

to beat off their rivals to build a line direct to Birmingham in 1852. GWR also built broad gauge tracks to Wolverhampton, although they used standard gauge for the line to Birkenhead.

The problem of broad and standard gauge however was solved, not by Parliament, GWR or Brunel, but by the Midland Railway, who eventually acquired the Bristol and Gloucester Railway, and built a third track so that standard or broad gauge locomotives and carriages could run on the lines. In 1861, the two great companies, GWR and Midland Railway merged and the gauge "wars" were over with many lines converted to standard gauge.

GWR, with its newly acquired Midland Railway, continued to flourish and Brunel remained an integral part of the mix. Standard gauge tracks were now being built as the norm, however, where broad gauge tracks remained, mixed gauge tracks were incorporated so that

standard gauge.

The differences in widths of gauges brought about operating difficulties and confusion which was eventually settled by a Gauge Commission which much preferred the idea of the standard gauge. But GWR had already commissioned the world's first operating telegraph line which ran from London Paddington to West Drayton and the company was undeterred by a parliamentary commission that denounced the size of the gauges. GWR found themselves in competition with the likes of the London and North West Railway but managed

locomotives of both standard and broad were able to run side by side. Tracks were extended into south Devon, over the River Tamar – by way of the Royal Albert Bridge – down through Cornwall eventually reaching Penzance in 1867. Brunel's bridge over the River Tamar is also known as a bowstring suspension bridge which is a simple, yet graceful, construction built by an engineer who was renowned for involving the most practical way of problem solving. The bridge is comprised of an iron arch or bow which is hung by suspension chains on each side of the tube. The railway itself is carried on a plate girder road and the bridge is based on the principle of a suspension bridge which makes it

LEFT Crowds on the banks of the River Tamar at Saltash, Cornwall celebrate the opening of the Royal Albert Bridge, 1859

ABOVE A GWR broad gauge locomotive at Swindon Station

unique even today as it is the only one of its kind to carry mainline trains. To compensate for the limitations of a suspension bridge each vertical is restrained through a system of diagonal bracing pinned at both ends to connect the main tube and the chain links.

Tracks were also laid to join with the South Wales Railway in 1850 via another of Brunel's railway bridges, the Wye, in 1852. In 1873, work on the Severn Tunnel commenced to allow a more direct route, but the engineering requirements and construction were difficult and costly and the tunnel remained unfinished and unopened until 1886. By the end of the 1800s, all broad gauge tracks had been replaced by standard gauge lines. New locomotives were introduced on the network and this is where the Star class, the

Saint class and the 2800 class locomotives were developed. However, not all that happened for GWR was positive and in 1923 the company came under the government who decided to amalgamate the railways into four main groups. But, GWR was the only railway company to maintain its identity at the end of World War I and it gained almost another 1,000 miles in line with the companies that were merged into it, taking the total length of the company's lines to almost 4,000 miles. GWR became part of the nationalised British Railways on 1 January 1948.

BELOW Men working on the construction of the Severn Tunnel

Southern

SOUTHERN RAILWAY, SR, CAME into operation in 1921 with the grouping of the railways following the Railways Act. A number of companies were amalgamated including the London and South Western Railway with the London, Brighton and South Coast Railway, the London, Chatham and Dover Railway and the South Eastern Railway. Competition from other modes of transport, including cars and particularly buses, had developed dramatically at the end of World War I which was further compounded by the formation of national bus companies at the end of the 1920s.

The railways in Devon were hit particularly hard and the introduction of the Western National Omnibus Company in 1929 which operated in the GWR region was a pressure that the railways could have done without. Branch lines were lost to competition and in Devon the Plymouth to Yealmpton was one of the first to close on 7 July 1930. Mainline stations were also hit and this meant closures. Sites,

RIGHT Workmen putting the finishing touches to a locomotive in the Southern Railway works at Eastleigh, Hampshire, 1933

including the wagon lift on the quayside at Calstock Station were sold off as former services were no longer required. And, in 1934, Southern Railway's own locomotive Lord Hood was brought down to the Plymouth area via GWR lines as it was prohibited from travelling on its own company's tracks.

However, there were developments

in other areas and in 1938 the Royal Naval Armament Depot at Ernesettle (an area of Plymouth) was connected via the Southern Railway between St Budeaux station and Tamerton Foliot. This development was initially brought about by the threat of another world war as previous plans to connect the GWR and SR at St Budeaux – made in 1919 – for the transport of goods between the two railways, the Plymouth dockyard and the armament depot, were almost long forgotten. From 1 September 1939, with World War II looming, railways were once again brought under government control. The war brought a great deal of activity to Southern Railway in Devon and in 1940 a munitions siding became operational next to Friary A signal box. Plymouth was a regular target for enemy bombers and in November 1941 the branch line to Yealmpton was re-opened while numerous smaller abandoned stations, including Lucas Terrace Halt, were once again part of operations.

Meanwhile, the Somerset and Dorset Joint Railway, founded in 1875, was also at the cen-tre of change during the time that Southern Railways were operational serving a rural, sparsely populated area along a seven and a half mile stretch from Bath to Broadstone and on to Bournemouth West. There were branch lines to Bridgwater, Burnham-on-Sea and Wells while the main line itself was renowned for its steep gradients and long patches of single track crossing the Mendip Hills. This caused severe double heading – the use of two loco-motives to pull the carriages – and an increase in costs, and the Somerset and Dorset line coined the name "Slow and Dirty". However, other parts of the railway, including the branch line to Burnham-on-Sea, were straightfor-

RIGHT A 2-4-0 type
locomotive built
for the Somerset &
Dorset Railway

ward and flat. The best known train on this former line was the Pines Express – officially named in 1927 – which was regularly used for the traverse trip from Bournemouth to Bath and on to Birmingham, Manchester, Liverpool and Sheffield. Southern operated south of Bath (Midland Railway operated north of the city), but overlapping of territory was common.

Many of the locomotives used on this part of the Southern line were Somerset and Dorset 7Fs, six of which were built in 1914 by Midland, but in 1925 a further five were built by Robert Stephenson and Company which were mainly goods trains. Excellent with heavy goods, these locomotives would also pull passenger carriages during busier periods. After the railways were nationalised in 1948, this line was given to the Southern Region but from 1958 was operated by Western Region and things were never the same again. The company announced in 1962 that the line would operate as a local route and much of the goods traffic was lost. The last route was taken on the Somerset and

Dorset line by Evening Star. The demise of the Somerset coalfields, the need for double heading and the loss of other goods traffic led to the lines' downfall.

Another line that was affected by the Southern line was the Dartmoor Railway, originally incorporated into the Okehampton Railway Company by the Okehampton Railway Act in 1862. It became part of Southern Railway in 1923 when it was by then a part of LSWR. This stretch of line was a competitive link to the South Devon line via Newton Abbot and Totnes for almost 90 years. Originally, the line formed the

the Plymouth area with its Devon and Cornwall Railway. The Dartmoor line began construction in Colebrook and stretched to North Tawton opening in 1865. A further stretch to Sampford Courtenay opened in 1867 where the main terminus remained until 1871 when the line finally reached Okehampton itself. The line to Lydford began construction in 1869 and this, along with the Holsworthy line, became a part of the LSWR but the latter line was not completed until 1898 when it finally reached Bude on the north Cornwall coast. Also in north Cornwall, a line was built from Launceston to Wadebridge and was then connected to the Bodmin and Wadebridge Railway (also acquired by the LSWR).

LSWR became part of Southern Railway in the amalgamation of the railways in 1923. Western Region took over the lines in the area under British Railways in 1963 and much of the system was downgraded. As a result, the report by Dr Richard Beeching signalled the end for much of this network and most of it was ultimately closed in the late 1960s.

critical link and was part of the line that fed into the junction built at Exeter which also included a track to Barnstable on the North Devon Railway and to Okehampton, while other lines were then built to Lydford to connect with the Launceston and South Devon Railway, to Bude in Cornwall and Torrington in Devon.

The Dartmoor Railway offered the former London and South Western Railway the opportunity to cover much sought after ground with stiff competition from the Great Western Railway who decidedly had the monopoly. The company was keen to move into

LMS

THE LONDON MIDLAND AND Scottish Railway was one of the "big" four created by the grouping of the Railways Act in 1923. The new group was an amalgamation of the Caledonian Railway, the Furness Railway, the Glasgow and South Western Railway, the Highland Railway, the London and North Western Railway, the Midland Railway and the North Staffordshire Railway as well as numerous subsidiary railways which were leased or

RIGHT Economist and chairman of the LMS, Sir Josiah Stamp, riding a model railway engine

maintained by these companies. The main London Midland and Scottish routes were along the west Coast with the Midland main line servicing the Midlands, the northwest, Scotland and London while the company's main business was freight transportation between major industrial centres.

The company's early history was dominated by in-fighting which led to Josiah Stamp bringing in a new chief mechanical engineer, William Stanier, in 1933. A shrewd man, Stamp had entered the civil service as a clerk in the Inland Revenue while he studied for a degree in economics. By the age of 23, Stamp was assistant inspector of taxes in Hereford and by 36 was assistant secretary to the Board of the Inland Revenue. As one of the UK's leading economists, Stamp left the civil service to become a businessman and in 1926 became the first president of LMS, however the railways were not Stamp's forte and like Dr Beeching he believed that there was only one way to approach a huge business venture. It was his biggest shortfall as he failed to see that the railway depended largely on its staff and that their commitment, dedication and morale were crucial to the success of the business.

Stanier on the other hand had the railway in his blood having followed his father into a career with GWR in Swindon – where the locomotives for the line were worked on. He worked initially as a draughtsman before becoming inspector of materials in 1900. The great engineer George Churchward employed him as a divisional locomotive superintendent and he returned to his native Swindon in 1912 to become assistant works manager before gaining promotion to the top job some eight years later. Josiah Stamp may not have understood the diverse range of management needed for his railway, but he did understand the need for professional help and he poached Stanier to join LMS from GWR.

Stanier was instrumental in putting the company back on track and quickly dispelled the trouble between the two factions – mainly from the former Midland Railway and the North

ABOVE A signwriter renewing the LMS crest on the side of one of its carriages

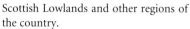

ABOVE The front of a pair of LMS steam engines saved for preservation; the "Hardwicke" alongside the Caledonian railway locomotive "No 123"

BELOW Engineer and surveyor Joseph Locke

Scottish Lowlands and other regions of the country.

Traditionally, the railways in Scotland were unconnected and links to England and in particular London meant long journeys by sea and rail before the Caledonian Railway was incorporated. When building a link with Carlisle, engineer Joseph Locke was persuaded to survey the route through Annandale and Clydesdale, although he felt that the gradients in stretches of the route would be too steep for locomotives. When the eventual line opened in 1849 it cut travelling time between London and Glasgow by hours to just more than 12 with its main line running from Carlisle, via Annandale and Clydesdale to Glasgow direct. This line is still in use today and it is now the north section of the West Coast Main Line. Many of the former stations have closed.

Like the Caledonian Railway, the North Staffordshire Railway became a part of the regrouping of the railways in 1923 when more than 300 incorporated railways were reduced to just four. Incorporated in 1845, the company began amalgamating former smaller railways and other businesses into its network including the Trent and Mersey Canal – which it leased

Western Railway – by introducing new ideas rather than trying to maintain two "old" distinct types of working.

The Caledonian line was a major Scottish railway before becoming part of LMS, operating exclusively in Scotland for the best part of 100 years. Its railway works were located in Glasgow which are still in use today and the company's principal objective was to link local railways around the major cities of Edinburgh and Glasgow and to connect Scotland to England via the railway at Carlisle. Additional lines later in Caledonian's history included links to Sterling, Aberdeen, Perth and Dundee while it competed with other Scottish railways for the

from 1846 – and the Derby and Crewe Railway. The company also undertook to build railway lines including a line from Macclesfield to Crewe and another from Harecastle to Sandbach to name a few. Chairman of the NSR, John L Ricardo, also a MP, oversaw the official ceremony to mark the occasion of construction getting underway and by 1847 nearly 1,500 workers had made great strides with the route between Macclesfield and Colwich on the way to Crewe. Passengers were able to take advantage of the railway's services by 1848 and line construction across the NSR region continued apace until the early 1900s.

The Glasgow and South Western Railway was formed in 1843 when it took over the railway between Dalry and Kilmarnock. The company slowly acquired other lines over the next seven years including the Irvine to Crosshouse, the Kilmarnock to Muirkirk and Galston, and the Dumfries to Gretna Junction as well as the New Cumnock to Closeburn and Auchinleck. It also took over the first ever Scottish railway, the Kilmarnock and Troon Railway which was incorporated in 1808. Like all other railway companies that were eventually taken over by one of the "big" four and then

nationalised as part of British Railways, the NSR suffered swift and rapid closures when the government's modernisation of the railways took place during the 1960s and 1970s. In 1966, the Bridge of Weir Railway and the Greenock and Ayrshire Railway was closed between Princes Pier and Kilmacolm, while the Paisley Canal station became a restaurant and the line beyond Paisley became a foot and cycle path.

BELOW The London Midland and Scottish Railway locomotive "Fury" at the Hyde Park works in Glasgow

LNER

SIR RALPH WEDGWOOD WAS THE chief general manager of the London and North Eastern Railway, the second largest of the "big" four brought about by the Railways Act of 1921. Sir Ralph (1874-1956) was a pioneer of LNER for the company's first 16 years from its inauguration in 1923. Coming from an influential family – his great-uncle by marriage was Charles Darwin, while his own great-great grandfather was pottery baron Josiah Wedgwood – Sir Ralph joined North Eastern Railway having developed a huge interest and deep affection for steam locomotives. Railways, like they were for William Stanier, were in his blood and he quickly became a district superintendent in 1902 becoming secretary two years later. Wedgwood successfully established himself in many roles for NER including passenger manager, deputy general manager and goods manager before

RIGHT "Silverlink", an LNER engine

he volunteered for service in World War I.

He became director of docks in 1916 with the rank of Brigadier-General but he returned to NER three years later and succeeded Sir Alexander Butterworth as general manager some three years after that in 1922. A year later when LNER was formed, Sir Ralph, became

BUTLIN'S HOLIDAY CAMP SKEGNESS
IT'S QUICKER BY RAIL

the first chief of the company in 1923. Wedgwood's forte was running this huge company and he was somewhat awe-inspiring to those who worked with him. Combined with the fact that this great man's heart was with the railways it was a winning combination that made LNER a success and his early days learning about the railways were never forgotten or taken for granted.

The tough, practical experience he had gained at the beginning of his career with railway traffic while working on the docks at Teesside gave the experienced Wedgwood the know-how, aptitude and ability to deal with every facet that he dealt with in his role as general manager and to understand the intricate details that his deputy managers were bringing to him. After his retirement, Sir Ralph Wedgwood was approached by the government to chair the Railway Executive Committee at the onset of World War II and to manage the railway networks across the country.

Under Sir Ralph's guidance and expertise, LNER itself prospered and was devoid of the infighting and troubles that seemed to trouble other railways covering the north and east of London. The company was made up of the former Great Eastern Railway, the Great Central Railway, the Great Northern Railway, the Great North of Scotland Railway, the Hull and Barnsley Railway, the North British Railway and the North Eastern Railway and had a total route of nearly 7,000 miles. The stock

RIGHT An LNER locomotive passing a signal point

and freight along with other assets the company owned were phenomenal for the time and included more than 7,650 locomotives, 20,000 coaches, nearly 30,000 freight vehicles, 140 electric rolling stock, six electric locomotives and 10 rail cars. The company also owned 36 steamers, river boats and lake steamers along with six turbines, 23 hotels, piers, docks and harbours (across 20 locations) and in partnership with the LMSR was co-owner of the Midland and Great Northern Joint Railway which was the UK's largest joint railway. This however was incorporated into LNER in 1936. The main routes

of the LNER were the East Coast Main Line which stretched from London to Edinburgh calling at York and Newcastle upon Tyne and routes from Edinburgh to Aberdeen and Inverness. With its main workshops located in Doncaster, just north of another of the company's regions, East Anglia, LNER dominated most of the country east of the Pennines.

Sir Nigel Gresley, the man responsible for so many successful locomotives and their outstanding performances, was a personal friend and chief engineer for Sir Ralph Wedgwood who stayed with LNER for most of the company's

rier in 1904, the Flying Scotsman was the first official train to reach speeds of more than 100mph while the Mallard holds the record for being the fastest steam locomotive in the world when it reached 126mph. Gresley was also responsible for designing the Gresley conjugated valve gear which involved only two sets of Walschaerts valve gear – a radial gear driving the wheel – which produced smoother running at high speeds on passenger trains and brought down running costs.

Another mechanic with LNER was Edward Thompson although his time with the company was short-lived and somewhat controversial. It was thought that some of Thompson's decisions were based on his dislike of Sir Nigel Gresley, although he was renowned for his dependable freight and mixed-traffic locomotives during wartime conditions. Serving only 18 months before nationalisation of the railways, Arthur Peppercorn, another notable designer for the company managed to bring in the A1 and A2 Pacific designs which were express passenger locomotives. He was an admirer of Gresley and despite his short time with LNER brought classic Gresley-like locomotives

existence. Nigel Gresley had previously worked for Great Northern Railway (GNR) where he had also been chief mechanical engineer. Gresley designed some of the most famous locomotives in the UK including the LNER Class A3 (including the Flying Scotsman) and the LNER Class A4 (including the Mallard). Both these trains were designed and built for speed and although the City of Truro broke the 100mph speed bar-to the company that had more reliability and solidity than those of his mentor.

Of the former companies that made up LNER in 1923, Great Eastern Railways (GER) was formed in 1862 with the amalgamation of the Eastern Counties Railway, the Norfolk Railway, the Eastern Union Railway, the Newmarket Railway, the Harwich Railway, the East Anglian Light Railway and the East Suffolk Railway. The Great Central Railway (GCR) ran from Manchester to Sheffield, Grimsby and Cleethorpes with an alternative route running from Barnsley, Doncaster and Scunthorpe to Grimsby while the Great North of Scotland Railway served the north east of Scotland from Aberdeen to Elgin serving mainly agricultural areas. Eventually becoming a main part of the East Coast Main Line, the Great Northern Railway headed north from London via Peter-borough, Grantham and York with branch lines to Sheffield and Wakefield as well as Boston and

Lincoln while the North British Railway operated between Edinburgh, Glasgow, Carlisle, Newcastle upon Tyne and Aberdeen.

LNER was nationalised in 1948 along with the rest of the railways under the Transport Act of 1947. British Railways was privatised in 1994 and the East Coast Main Line was taken over and renamed Great North Eastern Railways (GNER).

BELOW The driver and fireman of the Mallard checking the instrumentation after the record breaking feat

Settle and Carlisle

THE MIDLAND RAILWAY COM-PANY built the Settle and Carlisle rail-way between 1870 and 1876 after a dispute over access to Scotland with the London and North Western Railway. Both the East Coast Main Line and the West Coast Main Line were estab-lished and served passengers between England and beyond the Scottish bor-der while the Midland Railway faced fierce competition and was struggling to gain any co-operation from its rivals. The Midland was able to venture as far north as Ingleton in the Yorkshire Dales and requests to transport both the company's passengers and freight further north were not particularly well received.

By 1865 the company had had enough of its unhelpful contemporar-ies and applied to Parliament to carry out its own construction of a line which was duly passed. Passing through the foothills of the Pennines and treated as a main line, not a branch line, the newly constructed railway was devised as a competitive route for passengers, but things were not quite as well thought out as they might have been and some areas, including Dent, have stations that are at least four miles away from the community that they were built to serve. However to be fair, the Midland Railway had not initially intended the line to be a passenger line at the outset and had made no provision for sta-tions believing that the line would best serve the Scottish goods traffic of the time. However, considering that some stations were not even built when the line opened and others were still under construction, it is amazing to think that eventually this main line better served the passengers that used it more than other main lines with intricate and carefully thought out buildings, stations and accommodation.

The Settle and Carlisle route con-sisted of more than 70 miles of tracks and comprised 17 viaducts and 14 tun-nels. It was sold to potential customers as being the most scenic route through Scotland. These customers were keen on the idea of a picturesque route to Scotland and it became instrumental in the railway's success. It took around

6,000 men to construct the line using little more than dynamite, muscle power and temporary trams to build what was effectively the last man-made railway line in the country.

Hundreds of men were killed during construction although accidents were not the only reason for the high numbers as some fell foul of smallpox outbreaks while others were killed by fighting that broke out among the navvies. However, accidents on the then Batty Moss (now Ribblehead) viaduct which comprised 24 stone arches of

BELOW Ribblehead viaduct on the Settle to Carlisle route

RIGHT The gothically inspired St Pancras Station

more than 32 metres high and 402 metres wide above the North Yorkshire moors caused such a loss of life that the Midland Railway were forced to pay for the cemetery at Chapel-le-Dale to be extended. Memorials are built along the line to remember all those who died building the line. More than 2,000 navvies had set up shanty towns on the moors while the viaduct was built and it is one of the longest, highest and most famous of all viaducts. The viaduct took four years to build and is located at the foot of the Whernside mountain. (British Rail attempted to close the line over the viaduct in the 1980s citing that the viaduct was unstable. The plan was thwarted when trains were only allowed to cross singly and the line was saved and the viaduct confirmed structurally sound after extensive repairs.)

The Midland Railway specified that

gradients should be no more than one in 100 and the line quickly became coined the "long drag". Wanting to compete effectively for passengers, the company also stated that the line should be fast – hence the lower gradients – and that the buildings on the line's route should have an identity. All buildings featured the "Derby Gothic" resembling the gothic designs of the city – which is also in evidence at London St Pancras station – and were designed by John Holloway Sanders who worked on stations, buildings and houses where much of his work is still intact today – something that is fairly unique compared with many of today's railways. The idea was to impress whether the building was a station or workers' cottages and the architect has managed just that.

As well as having been a great feat of engineering, the line was planned down to the finest detail in its accommodation necessary for a main line despite the fact that many were not even started by the time the line opened. Facilities when stations did eventually materialise were well thought out and as a result few alterations or additional facilities have had to be added over the years. The buildings went on to become as much a hallmark of the line as the route, viaducts and tunnels themselves. The Midland became an important employer in the region and built more than 150 houses and dwellings for its workers who were helping to aid the local agricultural and mineral industries

by providing a transportation system that could encourage and maintain the growth of local businesses.

The line officially opened in May 1876 and survived intact for the best part of 100 years before the Beeching Axe during the 1960s saw the minor stations closed as part of the government's reforms of the railways. The passenger stopping service was cut drastically and the line suffered a lack of investment for two decades. British Railways announced that it would close the line during the 1980s and a campaign began to save the railway and uncovered some of the less scrupulous ploys that the national company were employing in their attempt to see the historic line closed for good. It took until the end of that decade for BR to agree to keep the line open while also agreeing to carry out necessary repairs and structural work on various parts of the line.

The 1980s saw a shift in freight traffic on the line from the Settle and Carlisle railway to the West Coast Main Line. However, increased traffic on the main line has seen the return of some freight to the Settle and Carlisle line again and in addition, passenger traffic has also increased and even some minor stations have been re-opened.

Stockton & Darlington

THE FIRST PERMANENT STEAM locomotive railway was the Stockton and Darlington Railway which opened in 1825. The railway was the idea of local businessman Edward Pease who as a wool merchant – he had gone to work for his father in the family business at aged 14 – was keen to develop transportation systems in the local area having recognised the need for a railway to carry coal from the collieries of West Durham to Stockton-on-Tees. The idea originally was to use a horse-drawn carriage as was typical of the time but, after Parliament passed a bill allowing the railway to be built in 1821, plans changed.

The legendary George Stephenson had already built the Hetton Colliery Railway having spent the previous eight years or so perfecting his steam locomotives and he persuaded Pease to allow him to re-survey the route and look at the possibility of at least having some of the railway serviced by steam. A revised Act of Parliament was granted and Stephenson's recommendations were incorporated. At the time, although the bill included provisions for passengers, it was decidedly a minor part of the amended proposal.

Having formed the Stockton and Darlington Railway in 1821 with a group of like-minded businessmen, Pease was impressed with Stephenson's plans and gave him the post of chief engineer on the railway. A further company was formed in 1823 by Pease, Stephenson, his son Robert Stephenson and Michael Longridge – a major driving force in locomotive manufacture – to make locomotives specifically for the line. The company, named Robert Stephenson and Company set up its headquarters in Newcastle upon Tyne. Stephenson had abandoned the "steam springs" that had proved unsuccessful in his previous manipulations of his steam locomotives although he still used direct connection of the pistons by crank rods.

Timothy Hackworth, another pioneer of the steam locomotive, was brought in by Stephenson senior to work on the first successful train called Locomotion which was finished in 1825. It was

Hackman who suggested that coupling the wheels of this locomotive and its three successors with outside rods and return cranks instead of chains would make the engines more efficient and reliable. Due to the death of his son, Isaac, Pease missed the opening celebrations of the railway on 27 September 1825. Another of Pease's sons however did follow his father into the railways and when Pease retired Joseph Pease expanded his father's business and went on to become the largest colliery owner in the South Durham coalfield.

At 26 miles long, the route was built between Darlington and Stockton-on-Tees and branched out from Darlington to collieries in the northeast of the UK. Initially developed as a connection between inland coal mines and

LEFT George Stephenson's first successful steam engine, the property of Hetton Colliery

Stockton-on-Tees, where ships were waiting to transport the coal, the line also had a short horse-drawn section – as set out in the original Parliamentary bill – as well as locomotives from Robert Stephenson and Company and included

one of the first ever railway bridges designed by Ignatius Bonomi. Called the Skerne Bridge (near Darlington), it is the oldest railway bridge still in use today while the track itself is standard gauge and was probably responsible for standard gauge being set at 1,435mm as this was necessary on the Stockton and Darlington Railway to accommodate the horse-drawn wagons on the older parts of the route serving the coal mines. Horses dominated the railways for the early part of the railway's history on the Stockton and Darlington until steam locomotives could prove their usefulness.

Many were unconvinced by the use of steam and due to the expense, unreliability and untried effects of steam – which innovators were striving to perfect – horses were very much a part of life on the railway. Locomotion No 1 was the first steam engine to run on the railway and at the official opening

– missed by Pease – the locomotive carried nearly 600 passengers on its maiden journey. It took two hours to travel 12 miles while most passengers were seated in coal wagons, however another coach called "The Experiment" was built like a wooden shed and carried a number of dignitaries for the occasion.

Although run as an experiment, a regular passenger service on the line was established, initially with a horse-drawn coach while meanwhile, Stephenson and Company were working on three more locomotives. Stephenson introduced his Experiment in 1826 which incorporated inclined cylinders that could be mounted on springs – originally four-wheeled the locomotive now had six wheels. Early designs, including those from other engineers, were not particularly successful and Hackworth was charged with producing an improved design. The following year, 1827, saw the pioneer unveil the Royal George with its spring-loaded safety valve to alleviate the need for drivers to tie the valves down in case they went over a bump.

Due to expert design and improved modifications, steam was beginning to triumph over the horse and within a relatively short time locomotives were beginning to prove their increased reliability and economic values. They could pull more, go faster and as more and more locomotives hit the railways, horses that were somewhat slower than the new technology gradually began to be overlooked in favour of the modern era. Originally the Stockton and Darlington railway did not operate the actual locomotives themselves and any paying party could freely operate on the line but fights over rights of way were common and the situation became intolerable for all and entirely unworkable.

New methods of operating the railways were devised and by the time that the Stockton and Darlington Railway was completely driven by steam locomotives the company was in sole charge of the line and those who relied on it. By 1833 the line began to resemble a modern railway and parallel tracks were built allowing for two-way traffic, timetables were established and a signalling system of sorts was devised to protect all those using the railway and to prevent collisions. The venture was an incredible success and is responsible for the way that modern railways are still run today.

Chapter 6

Famous Trains

Mallard

NAMED BY ITS FAMOUS DESIGNER, Sir Nigel Gresley, who came up with the name while feeding ducks, the Mallard set the world speed record for a steam locomotive on 3 July 1938 when it was recorded travelling at 126mph. Costing LNER £8,500, the Mallard is a LNER 4-6-2-A4 class and was given the number 4468. Gresley, chief mechanical engineer for the railway company for most of his working life, built the train in Doncaster in the early 1930s. Like all rail companies during the 1930s, LNER was facing stiff competition from road transport – particularly buses – and air travel, and there was increasing pressure on engineers such as Gresley to

design faster, more reliable locomotives and carriages to combat the fear of the railway's demise.

Trains in Europe and the US, including the diesel-electric Fliegende Hamburger of the German State Railways and the Burlington Zephyr from the US were somehow making the UK's steam traction engines look dated and slow and Gresley decided to take a look at streamlining his A3 model. The A3 had originally been more reliable than some of Gresley's other designs, but something more streamlined was now required to compete with the headlines that trains overseas were receiving. The Flying Scotsman, the engineer's A1 class design had reached 100mph during trials while his Papyrus A3 engine was said to have achieved 108mph.

Gresley was commissioned by his

company to take his streamlining ideas from the drawing board to the workshop and after long trials involving wind tunnel testing he devised the A4 class. There was fierce criticism for the job that the experienced engineer

new "super-powered" steam locomotive was held on 27 September 1935 when the train travelled from London King's Cross to Grantham touching 112mph. The crew were unaware of this record-breaking speed and Gresley had to inform them that they were making the passengers nervous after which the train slowed to a more moderate speed.

The Mallard first came into service officially later that same year and three further locomotives were built to run in conjunction with the formative engine on the new Silver Jubilee service to Newcastle upon Tyne. The speed of the new A4 class engines cut journey times between Newcastle and London down to four hours and the route was a huge success with both LNER and passengers alike. Services were extended and a number of other A4s were built to cope with the demand. The UK's first inter-city network was born when these exceptional train services were then extended to Leeds and Bradford.

Like most things Gresley had done before, other engineers copied his pioneering ideas and it wasn't long before railway companies such as LMS with the Coronation class and Southern Railways with a new streamlined class were trying

was doing, but Gresley managed to streamline virtually every part of the train both inside and out. The casing was worked, the steam passages were streamlined and the boiler pressure was increased from 220psi to 250psi. Modifications based on the A3 were made and the inaugural run of this

to better the Mallard's 112mph record – it was beaten by an LMS Coronation class at 114mph. However, railway bosses were concerned about passenger safety and an agreement to put customers' safety first and to ensure slower speeds had to be adhered to.

Gresley was determined that one of his own trains should hold the fastest speed for a steam locomotive and the Mallard was chosen on a trip designed to test the brakes. Pulling out of Grantham station, the train headed south for King's Cross, and Gresley took his chance. The train reached 126mph before settling at around 120mph. The engine overheated and the train had to undergo repairs in Doncaster, however a commemorative plate was attached to the Mallard's footplate to keep its record prominent for posterity.

The train was withdrawn from service in 1963 and is now on display at the National Railway Museum in York.

BELOW The Mallard at rest

The Flying Scotsman

PERHAPS THE FLYING SCOTSMAN is the most famous steam locomotive of them all. The 390-mile route still taken by this train between London King's Cross and Edinburgh now takes less than half the time it did when the train began its journey from London heading north back in the early 1900s. In 1924 when the railways were grouped under the Railway Groupings Act, the Special Scotch Express as it was then known became the pioneering brand of the London North Eastern Railway (LNER) who as one of the "big four" took responsibility for the route. The other three companies, including London Midland & Scottish Railway (LMSR), Great Western Railway (GWR) and Southern Railway (SR) did not have the same powerful marketing tool as LNER.

The economic depression of the 1930s was especially difficult, but the Flying Scotsman kept LNER firmly on the map by travelling non-stop between its two cities cutting its journey time from more than 10

BELOW The Flying Scotsman at Crewe

hours to seven hours and 20 minutes. And, by the end of the Depression, passengers were treated to luxuries such as an onboard hairdressing service, cocktail bar and fine cuisine. Despite the high-speed trains of today, the Flying Scotsman is still the most talked about train on the East Coast Main Line and all modern trains sport the words "The route of the Flying Scotsman" on their engines. Great North Eastern Railway (GNER) are as keen to promote their flagship train as LNER were all those years before them.

The Flying Scotsman was ready for service in February 1923 having been built in Doncaster. At a cost of £7,945, the train originally went on display at Marylebone before beginning its 80-year service as No 1472. After some repairs in 1924, the train

was re-numbered 4472 and with the help of chief mechanical engineer, Nigel Gresley, managed to run non-stop from London to Edinburgh on one tender of coal. Gresley was largely responsible for the Flying Scotsman's stunning performance – renamed in 1928 – and the train was so popular and so adored by the public that it was used in the film

ABOVE Passengers on the platform alongside the Flying Scotsman while she was still in service, 1935

The Flying Scotsman in 1929. Ten years later at the outbreak of World War II, the Flying Scotsman's role as flagship train, record breaker and movie star were put on hold as the engine was used to pull goods, carry parcels and transport passengers during the war years.

When British Railways came into being in 1948, there were no signs of re-establishing the Flying Scotsman as a leading light for the railways. In fact, after recommendations in Dr Richard Beeching's report on behalf of the government, the Flying Scotsman – along with many other steam locomotives – was due to finish service and head for the breaker's yard around 1955. Forward-thinking businessman and member of the Eastern Regional Board for British Railways, Alan Pegler, bought the Flying Scotsman and secured that the locomotive could be used on the network as a nostalgic passenger train. He paid £3,000 in 1963 for the legendary train and gave it a complete overhaul restoring it to its former glory. Pegler took the train on tour in the US but lost his fortune through paying for the costly trip. The Flying Scotsman was bought by William McAlpine and shipped back to the UK.

In 1988 the locomotive was on tour again, this time in Australia where it established the record for the longest non-stop run by a steam locomotive at 442 miles. The Flying Scotsman was set for a complete overhaul in 2007. It was bought for the nation three years previously and now resides at the National Railway Museum in York.

BELOW The Flying Scotsman at Doncaster

Duchess of Hamilton

around the boiler. It was shipped to New York a year after it was made,

THE DUCHESS OF HAMILTON IS A Princess Coronation Class 6229 that was built in 1938 in Crewe. The engine was the tenth in the class to be built and today is a preserved steam locomotive which until 2005 was sited at the National Railway Museum in York along with the Duchess of Sutherland and the City of Birmingham – also both preserved duchesses. Billy Butlin saved the train from the breaker's yard in Barry, South Wales, when he purchased the locomotive to become a playground attraction at one of his holiday camps where it survived before being loaned to the National Railway Museum by Butlins for 20 years from 1976. However the museum purchased the Duchess in 1987 and the train left service in 1996 when its licence finally expired.

Having been built as an express locomotive, the Duchess of Hamilton was an extremely modern looking locomotive with its streamlined casing

where it wowed the American crowds with its sleek lines and modern look.

Today, it is questionable whether this extra casing – resembling a bullet-shape

RIGHT The Coronation Scot was another locomotive in the streamlined Princess Coronation class

– actually did benefit the speed and performance of the engine but at the time it certainly looked as if it did and the class were renowned for being the fastest trains on the tracks anywhere in the country. The Princess Coronation class trains were the most powerful express passenger locomotives used in the UK working on the West Coast Main Line for the railway company LMS.

The engines were designed by renowned engineer William Stanier and were built for the London Midland and Scottish Railway (LMS) as an enlarged version of the LMS Princess Royal Class. The first five engines in the class were painted in the Caledonian Railway blue with silver stripes to match the Coronation Scot train that they were designed to haul in 1937. The next batch of five trains were also streamlined but were painted red in order to match new rolling stock, but the advent of World War II put paid to the building of more locomotives although several more were finished to help with the war effort and these were painted black.

Streamlining was removed on a permanent basis from the models built from 1946 onwards as the casing had been found to be little help when the engine was travelling below 90mph. The casing had also proved to be extremely unpopular with the maintenance staff and even those with casing intact had been stripped of it by 1949. Originally classified as a 7P in 1937, the locomotives were reclassified in 1951 as 8P. The first locomotive of this class to be built was the Coronation in June 1937 followed by the Queen Elizabeth, the Queen Mary, the Princess Alice and the Princess Alexandra (both in July 1937). A year later came the Duchess of Gloucester and the Duchess of Norfolk followed by the Duchess of Devonshire, the Duchess of Rutland and then the Duchess of Hamilton. The Duchess of Buccleuch was also a 1938 locomotive as was the Duchess of Atholl, the Duchess of Montrose, the Duchess of Sutherland and the Duchess of Abercorn. Today there are only six Duchess locomotives remaining.

A decision to restore the Duchess of Hamilton to the engine's original appearance with its streamlined casing was announced by the National Railway Museum in York in 2005 and work was completed in mid-2007 to coincide with the 70th anniversary of the Coronation Scot service for which the locomotive was originally built.

City of Truro

ALTHOUGH IT WAS NEVER OFFI-cially confirmed in the record books, the City of Truro was the first steam locomotive to exceed speeds of 100mph when it clocked up 102mph on 9 May 1904 pulling a mail train from Plymouth to London Paddington. Built in 1903 and designed by George Jackson Churchward, the City class, number 3440 – which was renumbered 3717 in 1912 – was renowned for its quick performance but as a smaller locomotive was taken off the main line as gradually more and more substantial engines were introduced.

Thirty years later, all the 4-4-0 steam locomotives were withdrawn from service, and the City of Truro was no exception. However in 1957, the steam locomotive was back in service – as number 3440 once again – at Didcot where it was used for special occasions on the Newbury and Southampton branch line in particular. When the City of Truro was finally retired in 1961, it was put on display at the National Railway Museum in York and in 2004 it was fully restored at a cost of in excess of £130,000 to mark the 100th anniversary of its record-breaking speed.

Built in Swindon by the Great Western Railway, it was not intended that the City of Truro should reach more than 100mph a year later as the top speed it was designed to manage was around 85mph. It was probably just insufficient training and bad manage-ment on the day that led to this train being the first to break the 100mph limit. Driven by train driver Clements and timed by Charles Rous-Marten, a writer for *The Railway Magazine*, the City of Truro left Millbay Crossing in Plymouth bound for Pylle Hill Junction in Bristol and made the 128-mile jour-ney in a record time of 123 minutes 19 seconds.

But the way in which the train was timed, how accu-rate the readings were and

whether mileposts had been misread all led to speculation about this class 4-4-0 and its ability to travel at such a high speed. Another obstacle that might reliably question whether the locomotive was able to reach 102mph was the steep climb to Whiteball where Rous-Marten as timer claimed the train was travelling at 62mph and then clocked up the record on the descent. Interestingly the magazine did not publish the record at the time, only the overall time of the journey. This was probably done to safeguard the publication's reputation although they did publish the 102mph in an article in 1907 – once the fuss had died down.

The available horsepower of the engine was called into question as the maximum indicated horsepower falls as a steam locomotive speeds past its peak.

LEFT The restored City of Truro passing through the Yorkshire countryside in 2004

The City of Truro would have needed 1,400ihp to make it to 102mph in less than three and a half miles and many believe that the 4-4-0 with its 1,000ihp could not have achieved the record its claimants made at the time. Experts have calculated since that the train may have reached 92mph but with a 148-ton train to haul this is just theory and the highest speed was likely to be 90mph. The claimed 102mph was nigh on impossible as far as some critics are concerned.

However, despite the lack of two time-keepers on the footplate to verify the speed and make the record official, Rous-Marten's timings past the mileposts do seem to have provided a record of consistency that is commensurate with a speed of 100mph or more. There were many inaccurate speed claims made both in the UK and the US which led to many of the earlier locomotives being saved from the breaker's yard when the days of steam ended – but that must surely be a good thing. Today there are stringent regulations for steam locomotives using the railways and so it is unlikely that anyone will ever be able to completely prove this dilemma one way or the other.

LEFT The Great Western Railway works in Swindon where the City of Truro was built

Evening Star

LIKE THE CITY OF TRURO, THE Evening Star was also built in Swindon, but arrived on the railways much later in March 1960. In fact, the Evening Star was the last steam locomotive built in the UK and was a class 2-10-0 numbered 92220. This train had a two-wheeled leading wagon with 10 driving wheels and was a 9F, highly powered engine, which was designed for freight rather than passengers. It was the only locomotive in its class to be given a name and unlike the other members of its class that were painted black, Evening Star was resplendent in livery green and boasted a double chimney that was copper-capped. Named by Mr K Grand – a member of the British Transport Commission – at a special naming ceremony, the train sported a commemorative name plate to mark the fact that it was the last steam locomotive built for British Railways. A competition had been held to name the last ever steam locomotive by the staff at the locomotive works in Swindon and the winning entry was based on the

ABOVE Evening Star
at Keighley

fact that one of the earliest locomotives had been named Morning Star. The judges decided that Evening Star was an appropriate name for a train that would see the end of the glory days of British steam.

The class 9F locomotives were specifically built for express freight transportation and had five coupled driving wheels that allowed for increased contact with the track making the steam traction engine strong and able to haul large and heavy freight. However, these trains were also capable of hauling express passenger trains and the Evening Star was stationed at Cardiff and was often used to haul the "Red Dragon" express to London. But class 9Fs were soon sent to the Somerset and Dorset Railway where they were used to haul both passenger and freight trains before the closure of the line. Before the demise of the Somerset and Dorset Railway in 1962, Evening Star was a regular feature and was the last steam locomotive to work on the line – even pulling the Pines Express that same year.

The rise of the Evening Star lasted for five short years before it faded into retirement in 1965. An accident had greatly contributed to the steam locomotive's withdrawal from service and it was also facing increased competition from diesel locomotives. It was, of course, up against the Beeching Report. Designers of the 9F locomotives were up in arms as they had specifically created engines to last for a 20-year period or more and many were destined never to pass their first decade. Despite this,

the 9F was one of the best steam locomotive designs that was ever built and was highly effective for the heavy loads for which it was designed to carry.

There are nine surviving 9F locomotives of which the Evening Star is one. The train went from service to preservation given its historical importance as the last locomotive to be built. The Evening Star is on display at the National Railway Museum in York. Another surviving 9F is the Black Prince, 92203, which was only named after preservation and not while working on the railways. Built a year before Evening Star in 1959, the Black Prince served nine years working for British Railways as a heavy iron ore train from Liverpool Docks to Shotton Steelworks. This purpose-built steam locomotive was the last steam traction to haul iron ore from the docks in 1967 before the newer, cheaper diesel locomotives took over. The train was bought from British Railways by artist David Shepherd and today is preserved at Gloucestershire and Warwickshire Railway. While in preservation the Black Prince set a record in 1983 for the heaviest train ever hauled by a steam traction engine in the UK when it pulled a 2,162-ton train in Somerset.

George Stephenson's Rocket

ALTHOUGH RICHARD TREVITHICK had spent a number of years developing a steam locomotive and was the first designer to put a traction engine on rails, it was George Stephenson who first came to prominence with his Rocket of 1829. Based on Stephenson's earlier designs – some of which had been heavily influenced by the less commercially successful Trevithick – the Rocket was the beginning of the evolution of steam and a forerunner of the "modern day" steam locomotives that worked across mainland Britain for the best part of a century.

Stephenson had been particularly interested in Trevithick's designs from the first time that he saw the Black Billy at Wylam in 1813. Almost entirely self-taught (he had been illiterate until early adulthood), Stephenson set about improving the early locomotive the following year at the Killingworth Colliery.

He quickly established himself as an innovator and successful businessman and his Locomotion engine was the first to work on a public steam railway – the Stockton and Darlington in 1825 – when he persuaded Edward Pease and his business associates of the Stockton and Darlington Railway to give steam a chance.

Although attributed to George Stephenson in the main, the Rocket was also designed by his son Robert – a co-founder of Robert Stephenson and Company based in Newcastle upon Tyne where the locomotive was built. What made the Rocket remarkable at the time was the design of a multi-tubular boiler which ensured the efficiency of the engine. This was somewhat revolutionary compared to earlier boilers that consisted of a single pipe surrounded by water. Other innovations of the Rocket included a vented exhaust system which allowed the steam up the chimney while fresh air was pulled into the fire thereby increasing both the heat of the fire and the pressure in the boiler, thus enabling the machine to move more quickly. The vent pipe was probably the brainchild of steam locomotive pioneer Timothy Hackworth who had been employed

LEFT George Stephenson's locomotive Rocket, constructed in 1829

by George Stephenson for his first class engineering skills. In addition, the Rocket was much lighter than its competitors and with one set of driving wheels was built for speed. This basic design was a revolution in steam locomotion and many designers following the Stephensons used this concept for their own innovations. With the advent of the Rocket, the beginnings of working steam locomotives had begun.

George Stephenson had designed and built his locomotive to compete in the Liverpool and Manchester Railway's Rainhill Trials in October 1829. The key requirement of the competition was to test the competing locomotives' abilities to complete a 50-mile round trip, hauling a load, while maintaining satisfactory fuel consumption. With 50 locomotives already designed, built and tested, the Stephenson family were fairly convinced of the Rocket's abilities.

One by one the other competitors broke down or pulled out of the race and the Rocket was declared the winner with an average speed of 12mph. Unloaded it was discovered that the Rocket could reach up to 29mph. The Liverpool and Manchester Railway, who had been using horse-drawn wagons on their railways, were delighted to commission eight locomotives from Robert Stephenson and Company while the company won £500 for winning the competition. The railway was officially opened 11 months later in 1830 but events were marred by the death of William Huskisson, the Liverpool MP, who became the railway's first fatality.

The Rocket was eventually sold to the Thompson family of Cumbria in 1836 and remained in service on the railways for a further four years. The family donated the locomotive to the Patent Museum in 1862.

Today, Stephenson's Rocket is on display with some modifications to the original as showcased at the Rainhill Trials at the Science Museum in London. A replica of the locomotive was built in 1979 to mark its 150th anniversary.

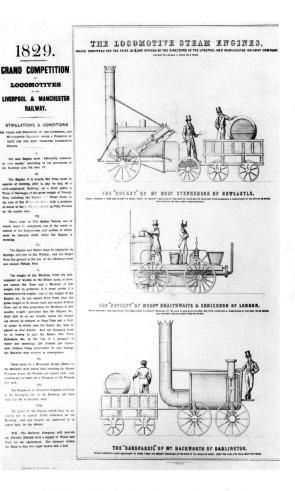

Princess Margaret Rose

THE LONDON MIDLAND AND Scottish Railway built engine 6203 at Crewe in 1935. The Princess Margaret Rose was classified as the Princess Royal Class and was the third steam locomotive of its type to be built. The locomotive was named after Princess Margaret Rose, the then five-year-old daughter of the Duke (later King George VI) and Duchess of York and sister of Queen Elizabeth II. The Princess Margaret Rose was renumbered 46203 when the railways were nationalised and remained in service until 1962.

The Princess Royal Class were express passenger trains designed by William Stanier with a 4-6-2 wheel arrangement with the specific task of hauling the Royal Scot train. This train ran between London Euston station and Glasgow starting in 1862 with earlier locomotives before the Princess Royal Class and the Princess Coronation Class took over the

journey. The Princess Royal class engines used steam turbines instead of cylinders until they became part of the huge modernisation of the railways from the early 1960s and were no longer required by British Railways.

Known by railwaymen as "Lizzies" after Princess Elizabeth before she became Queen, the class was developed into the quicker, sleeker, Princess Coronation Class which were designed and built in the late 1930s. The class was originally a 7P but was reclassified in 1951 to an 8P – where numbers 1-9 are used to describe the power of the engine with nine being the highest and the letter P meaning a passenger train. The class was built between 1933 and 1935 and only

12 locomotives of this type were commissioned. All the steam locomotives in the class were named after princesses who include the Princess Royal, Princess Elizabeth, Princess Louise, Princess Victoria, Princess Marie Louise, Princess Arthur of Connaught, Princess Helena Victoria, Princess Beatrice, Lady Patricia, Queen Maud, the Duchess of Kent and, of course, the Princess Margaret Rose. After retirement, the Princess Margaret Rose was bought by Billy Butlin for his holiday camp. The locomotive was restored at Crewe before moving to Pwlhelli in Gwynedd in 1963 where it remained until 1975. The steam locomotive was then sent to the Midland Railway Centre in Derbyshire as a display. Butlin's sold the Princess Margaret Rose for £60,000 in 1985 where restoration of this magnificent steam locomotive took place over a five-year period.

Today, only two Princess Royal Class steam locomotives are preserved, the Princess Margaret Rose and the Princess Elizabeth. The Princess Margaret Rose remains at the Midland Railway Centre where it is the property of the Princess Royal Locomotive Trust.

Knighted in 1944, Sir William Stanier, designer of the Princess Margaret Rose began his apprenticeship on the railways under William Dean on the Great Western Railway at Swindon. While in his native home town, Stanier also worked as principal assistant to chief mechanical engineer Charles Collett before moving to work with Josiah Stamp at the London Midland and Scottish Railway in 1932 where he remained until his retirement. On arriving at LMS Stanier discovered that the railway company had an acute shortage of heavy express passenger and freight locomotives which he then sought to provide through his designs.

More than 2,000 Stanier locomotives were built between 1932 and 1947. As well as the Princess Margaret Rose and the Princess Royal Class, Stanier was also responsible for designing the mixed traffic "Black Five" locomotives, considerable numbers of Class 8F engines, the Coronation class (introduced in 1937 and one of the most powerful locomotives ever to run on tracks in the UK), the Jubilee mixed traffic engines from 1934 and the rebuilding of Fowler's Royal Scot class.

LEFT The LMS engine Princess Royal getting up a head of steam as she leaves the station, 1933

Richard Trevithick's Penydarren tram road engine

RICHARD TREVITHICK, THE YOUNGest of six children, was born in Illogan, near Redruth in Cornwall in 1771. Born a mile from the coal mine where his father was a mine captain, Trevithick developed an interest and affinity for engineering at an early age. He was the first designer of a steam locomotive that ran on railway tracks and was a pioneer of the age of steam having studied all aspects of mine engineering at Camborne School of Mines. This led Trevithick to become responsible for the increased efficiency of engines pumping out water from Cornwall's tin and copper mines by advocating the use of high-pressure steam. His career came at the start of the industrial revolution when Cornwall's engineering abilities

in the mines was the envy of the world. It is probably true to say that Richard Trevithick had a healthy influence on developments at the time.

Strong and dependable – Trevithick had the reputation of being one of the best wrestlers in Cornwall – he went to work with his father at Wheal Treasury mine and, after making improvements to the Bull Steam Engine, became engineer at Ding Dong Mine in Penzance. Here he developed a successful highpressure engine that became in great demand in both Cornwall and South Wales for raising ore and refuse from mines. It was this success that gave Trevithick the idea of developing a steam locomotive and by 1796 he had created the first traction engine. By 1801 he had developed a much larger modified version of his first locomotive and he promptly took some friends on a short journey. By 1803 he had had a modicum of success in London and had even received backing for his experiments from Vivian & West but practical limitations saw the company withdraw from the project and Trevithick was forced to search elsewhere for support.

Samuel Homfray, the owner of the Penydarren Ironworks in Merthyr

Tydfil was a great admirer of Trevithick and commissioned the young engineer to try again. Previously, Homfray had made a 1,000 guineas bet with Richard Crawshay (owner of the Cyfarthfa Ironworks) that he would construct a steam locomotive to haul 10 tons of iron along a tramway to Abercynon. Crawshay accepted the bet and Trevithick set about designing a high-pressure tram-engine. The result in 1804 was the Penydarren locomotive – the first of its kind to successfully run on rails with its single vertical cylinder, long piston-rod and eight-foot flywheel that succeeded in hauling 10 tons of iron, 70 passengers and five wagons from the ironworks to the Merthyr-Cardiff canal.

Built in 1802, the Merthyr Tramway was jointly owned by the Dowlais, Penydarren and Plymouth ironworks. The journey was nine miles and the locomotive managed a top speed of five miles an hour. The rules of the wager were that Trevithick had to control and repair the locomotive unaided should any problems arise which they soon did when the Penydarren's chimney struck a low-level bridge and was destroyed. He duly cleared the debris and fixed the chimney before continuing on his journey which luckily proved uneventful. The loco-motive was unable to make the return journey due to the route's steep gradients and sharp corners despite the lack of a load. Most importantly of all the Penydarren had proved that steam locomotion was possible. The Penydarren only made three journeys as each time the locomotive broke the cast iron rails with its seven-ton weight. Homfray concluded that Trevithick's revolutionary invention was unlikely to save him transport costs and abandoned the project.

As a renowned engineer, Richard Trevithick was a forerunner for the modern world. His creative ideas ranged from the first successful self-powered road vehicle to steam locomotion, schemes for salvaging wrecks, land reclamation, mechanical refrigerators, agricultural machinery and engineering schemes for tunnelling under rivers.

ABOVE
Richard Trevithick

Stephenson's Locomotion No 1

STEPHENSON'S ENGINE LOCOMO-
tion was the first ever to work a
steam public railway which it did
on the Stockton and Darlington on
27 September 1825.
The locomotive was
a beam engine on wheels
with vertical cylinders
and coupling rods (as
designed by Timothy
Hackman) for its driv-
ing wheels rather than
chains. Despite its early
success Locomotion
No 1 quickly became
obsolete with the
advent of Stephenson's
Rocket while its
reputation was not
salvaged by the fact
that the boiler had
exploded three years
after its inaugural

BELOW Stephenson's
Locomotion No 1

trip, killing the driver. However, even
given the advances in steam locomotion,
this engine remained in service until 1841.

A replica of Locomotion No 1 was
built for the steam locomotive's 150th
anniversary in 1975 – and is now kept at
Beamish Museum – while the original
Stephenson design was preserved and is
now part of the National Collection and
is on loan from the National Railway
Museum in York at Darlington Railway
Centre and Museum.

Meanwhile, Locomotion No 1
and Stephenson's other early designs
brought about the formation of Robert
Stephenson and Company in 1823. The
company was located on Forth Street
in Newcastle upon Tyne and owned
by George and Robert Stephenson,
Edward Pease – the businessman behind
the Stockton and Darlington Railway
– and Michael Longridge, owner of
the Bedlington Ironworks. The reason for the company was to provide
the tracks, steam locomotives and carriages necessary to properly maintain
the Stockton and Darlington Railway
which George Stephenson had persuaded Edward Pease to allow steam
locomotives to run on. Locomotion No
1 was the first on the railway and was

followed by three more namely, Hope, Black Diamond and Diligence. Stability of these engines was less than reliable and Stephenson's introduction of "steam springs" also proved unsatisfactory. At this point the engineer developed a more stable locomotive and in 1828 the Experiment was launched on the railway proving itself more reliable with its mounted springs. A further locomotive, Victory, was built and the company expanded its empire by providing two steam locomotives bound for the US, one for the Delaware and Hudson Railroad and the other for the Boston and Providence Railroad called Whistler that was unfortunately lost on the journey across the Atlantic.

The company found great success with the Rocket's winning performance at the Rainhill Trials for the Liverpool and Manchester Railway who ordered eight locomotives to run on its railway. More locomotives were built and in the 1830s the company introduced the Planet class. Despite continuing success, the design of the locomotives were still proving problematic for the engineers and the railways' demands for increased mileage threw up issues over fireboxes and chimneys which were just not built to stand up to the increased pressure. Stephenson eventually trialled different chimneys and discovered that longer chimneys were necessary in order to combat the problems. With the new 4-2-0 design on the driving wheels performance was increased.

By now many other companies and engineers were springing up across the UK and the company faced increased competition. Based on the business acumen of all involved, however, the company continued to thrive for the remainder of the 1800s. By 1899 the company had built around 3,000 locomotives and a limited liability company was formed with new works in Darlington. Many of the larger companies were building their own locomotives and rolling stock so Robert Stephenson and Company found most of their customers overseas, including India and Argentina. The company turned to munitions work during World War I, but work was quiet on the whole. By 1937 the company merged to form Robert Stephenson and Hawthorns Limited. The last locomotives to be built by the company left the works in 1959.

King Edward I

STEAM LOCOMOTIVE 6024, KING Edward I, was a GWR King class four-cylinder 4-6-0 engine designed by Jackson Churchward, chief mechanical engineer at the railway company's works in Swindon. Under fierce competition from rival engineers at competing railway companies, Churchward was charged with designing a creative technologically-advanced locomotive. The engineer was renowned for constantly searching for innovative ideas for his designs and he found it in his four-cylinder King class locomotives which were arguably the most superior engines on the rail network during the early 20th century. However he didn't really see his dream materialise due to retirement.

His work was carried out by his successor, Charles Collett – mentor of William Stanier – who arrived at GWR to find standardised Swindon designs, but was faced with the task of rationalising the fleet and working on the under-investment that the company had suffered as a result of World War I. His first endeavour was to develop Churchward's two and four-cylinder designs. Directed by GWR's general manager Sir Felix Pole to come up with a larger, more efficient locomotive than had ever been seen before, Collett designed – with a little help from his predecessor – the King Class that appeared from the Swindon works in 1927 which had dimensions never seen previously.

The trains were heavy at 136 tons and were the largest locomotives in the UK. Thirty King class trains were built between 1927-28 and 1930 and the King Edward I was completed in the second batch of 10 locomotives at a cost of £7,500. The locomotive began work in July 1930 and averaged around 60,000 miles of service during its first five years. Its principal task was hauling the passenger express between London Paddington and the South West which it did until 1948 and the nationalisation of the railways.

After nationalisation, trials were carried out by British Railways to gauge the efficiency of the King Class and in 1953 King Edward I received a super-heater boiler after more than one million miles of service. The trials proved that the King Class were reliable, efficient, heavy load haulers who were able to cope with British Railways' new schedules with ease while maintaining speeds in excess of 90mph. They remained the dominant locomotives on the railways until the rise of faster diesel locomotives. All King class engines were fitted with new cylinders – the King Edward I receiving these in November 1957. King

Edward I ran for more than 30 years on the Great Western Railway and for the west region of British Railways regularly hauling the Cornish Riviera Express and the Bristolian and the Cambrian Coast Express. The King Edward I was renowned for its robustness and its longevity became legendary. The engine was never confined to secondary or minor duties during its service and was still working when the entire class was withdrawn from service in 1962.

The locomotive was sold to Woodham Brothers and sent to Barry in South Wales where it was due to be scrapped. However, the engine was saved from the breaker's yard by the

King Preservation Society in 1973 for £3,500 who planned to restore the locomotive to its former glory. The King Edward I was the thirty-sixth locomotive to be rescued from Barry and was taken to the Buckinghamshire Railway Centre where steady progress was made on its comeback aided by charitable funds. The work took the society more than 16 years but on 2 February 1989 the King Edward I once again took to the railway and was re-commissioned later that year by the Duke of Gloucester. It was back in service in 1990. The locomotive had been so painstakingly restored that it won the 1990 Heritage Reward (sponsored by British Coal).

U1 Garratt

LOCOMOTIVE NUMBER 2395, CLASS U1, was a lone engine designed by Sir Henry Fowler and built by Beyer Peacock to haul coal trains up a steeply graded line in South Yorkshire over the Worsborough Bank between Wentworth Junction and West Silkstone Junction. The steep incline was about three and a half miles long and had a gradient of one in 40. The engine was built in 1925 with three cylinders per engine and based on a LNER class Q4. Originally it was planned to build two of these engines, but only one ever left the locomotion works. Sir Nigel Gresley modified Fowler's design to include three cylinders and to use some of the

motion from the Q2 class. The train was first on display at the Stockton and Darlington Centenary celebration in July 1925 before being painted black and entering service in August that same year. The locomotive was the only Garrett to serve with LNER and was the most powerful engine of any type.

The train – the largest steam locomotive in the UK – would spend most of its time in the sidings on the Worsborough Bank waiting for the locomotives hauling around 60 or so coal wagons to arrive from Wath. Nicknamed the Wath Banker, the U1 would then leave the sidings and couple up behind the other locomotive. Once the load was taken off and the locomotives had reached Silkstone Junction, the U1 would then uncouple from the other locomotive and head back to

Wentworth Junction to wait for the next load. The Silkstone tunnels were extremely bad for the crew's health and the air quality was notoriously poor. In addition, corrosion of the U1's tubes were also a problem and just one year after entering service the engine had to be re-tubed. Then in 1928 the firebox was found to have corrosion and a chemical solution was introduced to alleviate the problem. But two years later, the locomotive spent the best part of the year out of service for reasons that have never been fully explained. The locomotive was re-numbered 9999 in 1946 but became number 69999 when British Railways took over the entire running of the railways in 1948 – despite this the engine kept the number plates with 2395 on the cab throughout its working life.

The locomotive required a new boiler in 1949, but it would only prove economical if alternative work was found for the engine as the lines between Manchester, Sheffield and Wath were about to be electrified. Luckily work was found on the Lickey Incline between 1949 and 1950 and then again in 1955. This was to be the locomotive's last job and it was withdrawn from service

later that same year after trials to oil conversion proved unsuccessful. The locomotive was not particularly popular with engine crews and was sent to be scrapped in 1955.

The U1, although a lone locomotive, was part of the wider class of Garratt engines built for London Midland and Scottish Railways for hauling heavy freight. There were 33 Garratts in total. Sir Henry Fowler who designed the U1 was chief mechanical engineer on the Midland Railway and later the London, Midland and Scottish Railway after regrouping in 1923. He began his career as a gas engineer on the L&YR in 1895, but by 1905 was assistant works manager and two years after that works manager for Midland Railway. One of his more famous designs, introduced in 1928, was the LMS Royal Scot 4-6-0 express locomotive that was based on Southern Railways' Lord Nelson Class. Beyer Peacock – the locomotive manufacturer – was responsible for building the U1 for LNER in 1925. Founded by Charles Beyer and Richard Peacock in 1854, the company's most important design was the Beyer-Garratt, an articulated locomotive which was used largely in Africa and Australia as well as the UK.

Green Arrow

THE GREEN ARROW – NUMBER 4771 – was designed and built by Sir Nigel Gresley in 1936 as part of London and North Eastern Railway's V2 steam locomotives. These engines were designed for mixed traffic – both passengers and freight – and the Green Arrow took its name after a freight service it provided. It was the first V2 class to be built and, interestingly, is the only surviving member of its class in existence today and is now part of the National Railway Collection at the National Railway Museum in York.

Constructed in Doncaster, the V2 class was based on the Class A1 and A2 Pacifics but had smaller driving wheels although the design incorporated Gresley's favoured three-cylinder arrangement and the wheel arrangement was 2-6-2 making the locomotives the first major class of its type in the UK. The wheel arrangement meant the introduction of a large firebox. Eleven batches of 184 V2s were built between 1936 and 1944 and unlike other locomotives that were put on hold during World War II, these engines

continued to be built as they proved their usefulness across the railway network. Only a few of the 184 V2s were named – the most famous being the Green Arrow – while the others included the Snapper, the Green Howard, St Peter's School York, Durham School, King's Own Yorkshire Light Infantry, Coldstreamer and the Durham Light Infantry.

The V2 class became LNER's most high profile mixed traffic design and put Sir Nigel Gresley's name on the railway map. The design can be traced back to 1932 and the modifications made to the K3 2-6-0 model, but the more favoured 2-6-2 arrangement took precedence in 1933 which allowed the traditional Gresley wide firebox to be fitted. The design was streamlined by 1934 and included a Kylchap exhaust, a rotary cam poppet valve gear and an ACFI feed water heater. The staff at the works were delighted with the design and the schedule was amended in 1935 to allow for 14 of the locomotives to be built for fast usage. The first five locomotives were ordered that same year although the final appearance had yet to be decided.

The A4 design was advocated as a possible design on which to base the V2s although a larger firebox was incorporated into the drawings showing a boiler one foot longer than the successful A4. The partially streamlined A4 cab was kept in the final draughts and the first locomotives were built in 1936 including the legendary Green Apple. V2s operated across the LNER region although most were kept in sheds along the East Coast Main Line between King's Cross London and Aberdeen. Green Arrow was posted to work out of King's Cross on the first leg of the journey to Glasgow for express freight. However, some V2s, having proved their adaptability, were also used in place of A1 and A3 Pacifics and sometimes instead of the highly streamlined A4s.

During World War II, many V2s – nicknamed "the locomotive that won the war" – were used to haul heavy passenger trains but throughout the war years maintenance of both the locomotives and the tracks suffered, leading to pins wearing out and lack of lubrication, so in 1946 one V2 had a mechanical lubricator fitted as a trial. Accidents however became rife with the V2s during 1946 involving derailment at excessive speeds. The pony truck also became an issue and these were replaced by 1947. The replacement of all pony trucks on V2s only led to one further derailment in 1952.

The V2 was gradually withdrawn from service from 1962 onwards and a total of 69 were off the railways by the end of the year. The last train to be taken out of service was number 60831 in December 1966 – it was the last of Gresley's large engines to be withdrawn.

BELOW Green Arrow

Chapter 7

Fictional Trains

STEAM LOCOMOTIVES ARE NOT just the reserve of the ardent "grown-up" enthusiast. Many children from tiny tots to awkward teenagers have an affinity for them through the likes of Thomas the Tank Engine and the Hogwarts Express. Through authors and film directors, the dreams of the older generation who believe that the importance of steam should be kept alive have come true with books, DVDs and films shown in cinema along with other activities involving steam trains which means that steam is enjoyed by young audiences worldwide.

BELOW Peter Fonda sits inside Thomas the Tank Engine during filming of *Thomas And The Magic Railroad*

Thomas the Tank Engine and Friends

FROM HUMBLE BEGINNINGS MORE than 60 years ago, Thomas the Tank Engine continues to be a hero for today's generation of toddlers. Enjoyed by girls and boys alike, this little steam locomotive and his friends are the brainchild of the Reverend Wilbert Awdry who began relating stories about the adventures of Thomas to his own son Christopher, having gained a passion for trains from his own father, the Reverend Vere Awdry as a young boy.

Railway stories first came to life for a wider audience in 1945 when the Reverend Awdry, encouraged by his wife, found a publisher for his book *The Three Railway Engines* featuring a story about Edward, Gordon and Henry. That same year Awdry made a small wooden toy engine that the young Awdry asked his father to make up stories about. The engine that Christopher called Thomas had a story published the following year called *Thomas the Tank Engine* and the rest, as they say, is history.

The success of Rev Awdry's books became a huge phenomenon. Due to the acclaim with which the stories were received, the parson created the fictional Island of Sodor where the trains could live and work while having their adventures. Later in life, Christopher Awdry began writing Thomas books himself to entertain his own son, Richard. His books were just as well received by a second generation of young Thomas fans who enjoyed the "Really Useful Engines" series.

Thomas was brought to millions of television screens – with voice-overs by the legendary Ringo Starr – by Britt Allcroft, an award-winning producer who had enjoyed the exploits of Thomas herself as a child. Allcroft was responsible for the first film *Thomas*

BELOW Ringo Starr, who voiced over the television series of *Thomas the Tank Engine*

and the Magic Railroad which hit the big screen in 2000 and starred Alec Baldwin as Mr Conductor and Peter Fonda as Burnett Stone.

Thomas, based on a South Coast Railway 0-6-0 E2, is renowned for getting into scrapes as the little steam locomotive who acts like a bigger engine – such as Gordon and James – but his heart is in the right place and he always makes good in the end. Two of Thomas's best friends are Bertie the Bus and Harold the Helicopter who are always there to help the engine out. Thomas looks up to the likes of Gordon, who despite being a superior, senior engine, is always willing to help smaller engines out of trouble and Henry, who underwent a re-model and is now extremely fast. Lady, another of the little engine's friends, is a special locomotive who only shows her face when running on the Island of Sodor. She also holds the secret to the Magic Railroad. There is always a "baddie" and in Thomas's world it's Diesel, or "Devious Diesel" as the other engines call him. Renowned for his scheming, conniving and annoying smirk, Diesel usually gets his comeuppance.

Hogwarts Express

THE ADVENTURES OF HARRY Potter, created by author JK Rowling, are an international phenomenon that came to life through the author's books based on witchcraft and wizardry. Each September, Harry and his other school friends are transported from platform 9¾ leaving London's King's Cross railway station bound for Hogwarts School on the fictional Hogwarts Express. Based on the concept of the 1930s and 1940s when steam locomotives were used by private schools to transport boarders, the train is a powerful red beast that is only visible to the students when they reach the platform through a magical barrier between platforms 9 and 10.

The Hogwarts Express first graced the screens throughout cinemas in *Harry Potter and the Philosopher's Stone* in 2001 when fans were overwhelmed by this adaptation of Rowling's first book. The train is the setting where Harry Potter, played by Daniel Radcliffe, meets his closest friends – Ron Weasley (Rupert Grint) and Hermione Granger

(Emma Watson) – for the first time. Hated by his Uncle Vernon, played by Richard Griffiths and Aunt Petunia (Fiona Shaw) it is always with some relief, and excitement, that Harry Potter boards the Hogwarts Express destined for Hogsmeade Station. To date, Harry Potter has found himself on the steam locomotive 10 times since starting his studies at Hogwart's to become a wizard.

The actual steam locomotive used in the film adaptations of the Harry Potter books is the Great Western Railway Hall Class 5972 Olton Hall. Director of the films, Chris Columbus, decided not to use the Southern Railway locomotive Taw Valley which was repainted and re-named temporarily for the films as he felt it was too modern looking.

JK Rowling has let it be known that the idea for Harry Potter came to her while on a train journey and so it seems rather fitting that the Hogwarts Express – the location for many scenes – is kept

central to the stories. However, the author was thinking of the layout of platforms 9 and 10 at Euston station rather than King's Cross when she wrote the books, but did not discover she had muddled up the stations until after the books were written. Of course, King's Cross station does not actually have a platform 9¾ although the station has used a building between its platforms to erect a platform 9¾ sign and has even gone as far as to have half a luggage trolley sticking out from the wall.

BELOW The platform sign for the Hogwarts Express

The Polar Express

IN 2004, THE BLOCKBUSTER FILM *The Polar Express* hit the big screens starring Tom Hanks who has no less than five parts in the movie. Based on the book of the same name that was published in 1998 by award winning author Chris Van Allsburg, it is an imaginative story which is fascinating, often mysterious and sometimes ironic. Born in Grand Rapids, Michigan in 1949, Van Allsburg is also an illustrator of children's books having studied art at the University of Michigan and an MFA from Rhode Island School of Design. Van Allsburg is also a triple Caldecott Honour Award winner – named after 19th century illustrator Randolph Caldecott – including for his first book *The Garden of Abdul Gasazi*, *Jumanji* and *The Polar Express*. The award is given annually by the Association for Library Service to Children to the illustrator who is deemed to have created the most brilliant American picture book.

Following in the footsteps of Jumanji that starred Robin Williams and Kirsten Dunst, The Polar Express was likewise adapted for the big screen. Directed by Robert Zemeckis, the film tells the story of a young boy who wakes on Christmas Eve to find a huge steam train "parked" outside his house. He

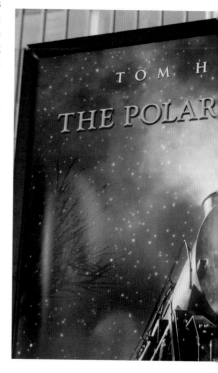

is given the chance to climb aboard by conductor Tom Hanks. This classic Christmas story is a heart-warming story about the boy who decides he will board the train, where most of the film is set, and his adventures along with other children on the way to the North Pole. As the hero boy, he meets up with a kind-hearted and thoughtful hero girl and a younger lonely boy. The magical train takes the children on a mysterious ride that throws up a variety of characters including the hobo – also played by Hanks in the movie.

When the train reaches the North Pole, Santa traditionally picks one child to ask him for a present before he makes his trip to fill all the Christmas stockings around the globe. He picks the hero boy who humbly asks for one of the bells from the reindeer's reigns. Santa grants him his wish, but the bell is lost before the train even leaves to take the children home. On Christmas morning there is a small present waiting for the boy under the tree which is, of course, his bell. He shakes the bell and it rings. This means that he truly believes in Santa. Cleverly animated, the film is a wonderful fairytale of mystery, intrigue and what if?

LEFT Tom Hanks, the star of the film *The Polar Express*, arriving at the premiere

Starlight Express

THIS PHENOMENAL WEST END show from composer Sir Andrew Lloyd Webber with lyrics by Richard Stilgoe became the second longest-running musical in London's theatre history in 1991. The concept for the idea was the brainchild of Lloyd Webber in 1975, although the award-winning composer had intended it to be an animated movie. Eight years later, Lloyd Webber rewrote the story for his children and *Starlight Express* was born.

The story about a group of trains, their relationships and struggles with each other is set on rollerskates while the cast whiz high above, below and around the audience for the entire show on cleverly built runs. This amazing spectacle involves the performers in dangerous stunts which is both exhilarating and breathtaking to watch. There are a number of trains featured in the story where one of the main central characters is Rusty, a steam locomotive who is shy and naïve. A favourite with audiences, Rusty is in love with Pearl, a carriage

who has trouble making up her mind over anything. Rusty loses Pearl and loses his confidence through his devastation. But, his father, Poppa, an

engine, is the fastest diesel locomotive in the world and defending speed racing champion. He taunts the little steam engine who is desperate to be as fast and courageous as his more modern rival. But even his friends – Ashley (smoking), Buffy (buffet) and Dinah (dining) don't support his quest for supremacy. The all-important race is announced and challengers, including Espresso from Italy and Nintendo from Japan turn out for the event. Each contender needs a carriage to race with them and Rusty finds he doesn't have one. After many races – and much cheating by unscrupulous contenders – Rusty, accompanied by Dustin (the heavyweight coal car) makes it over the finishing line first proving that old-fashioned craftsmanship can triumph over modern technology.

LEFT The rock musical *Starlight Express*

old retired steam engine comes out of retirement to show Rusty that power comes from within.

The arrogant Greaseball, a diesel

Chapter 8

World Famous Routes

THE OPPORTUNITY TO TRAVEL ON some of the most celebrated steam locomotives in the world is still available today for those seeking the excitement and thrill of days gone by.

Orient Express

DESPITE STARTING OUT AS A REGular service on 4 October 1883, the name the Orient Express is synonymous with luxury travel. The train was originally operated by the Compagnie Internationale des Wagons-Lit and on its inaugural journey travelled from Paris to Romania via Munich and Vienna. This first route also included transporting passengers from Giurgiu in Romania across the Danube to Bulgaria where they boarded another train bound for Varna in Bulgaria before the journey was completed by ferry

to Istanbul. Two years later another route was devised, this time reaching Istanbul by rail via Vienna, Belgrade and Plovdiv. Throughout the history of the Orient Express there have many different routes but sadly the route was discontinued from the summer of 2007 when the TGV – train à grande vitesse or high speed train – took over the direct rail line which was built direct to Istanbul in 1889.

From 1889, the Orient Express ran daily from the French capital to Budapest. It also had a timetable that mapped a route from Belgrade to Istanbul three times a week as well as travelling as far as the Black Sea once a week. Services were suspended at the start of World War I in 1914, as it was widely recognised that steam locomotives were not particularly good for fighting the enemy in the same way that aircraft and vehicles that could travel anywhere were. The train was operational again at the end of hostilities in 1918 and was now routed via Milan when the opening of the Simplon Tunnel the following year allowed an alternative train ride. This service ran in conjunction with the original routes and the Simplon Orient Express became the most important route between Paris and Istanbul. But it was the 1930s that were to prove the most important time for the steam locomotive and its services. By now there were many trains taking

different routes and it became a haven for the rich and famous and renowned for its quality service, fine cuisine and the introduction of sleeping cars.

The onset of another world war in 1939 once again saw services shut down and not resumed until the end of World War II in 1945. This was not without its problems as the Iron Curtain drew a tight reign across parts of Europe and communist nations insisted on using their own carriages to take over services at almost

LEFT An interior view of the Orient Express

BELOW A passenger boards the Orient Express during its journey through Yugoslavia on its way to Istanbul in the 1950s

every border. Only the Simplon Orient Express was running by the early 1960s which was itself replaced by the Direct Orient Express. In 1982 the Orient Express was established as a private venture and restored to its former glory as in the 1930s. Until its closure in 2007, the train had catered for passengers paying more than £1,000 each to travel between London, Paris and Venice on a weekly basis.

Trans-Siberian

DUBBED THE "JOURNEY OF A LIFE-time" by many who have experienced it, the Trans-Siberian Railway offers passengers the chance to travel across nine countries and nine different time zones on a 13-day excursion that trav-

RIGHT A locomotive from the fleet used to draw the Trans-Siberian Express through Russia, 1978

els the same distance as crossing the United States three times. The route connects Moscow and Eurasia with the far east of Russia, Mongolia, China and the Sea of Japan. With its main route running from Moscow to Vladivostok via Siberia, the Trans-Siberian Railway is steeped in history that dates back to 1891 when work on the railway began. Finished 25 years later, the route is in excess of 5,770 miles and is the third longest single continuous service across the globe. There are four main routes on the railway where the last, which runs further north than the others, was introduced as recently as 1991.

Siberia was decidedly undeveloped at the end of the 1800s partly due to a lack of transportation systems. Roads were few and rivers were the only real means of transportation – either by boat during the warmer months, or by a horse-drawn sled when the rivers had iced over during the harsh winter months. Encouraged by the Moscow/ St Petersburg Railway, efforts were made to encourage industry and the building of the railway in Siberia. By 1880 there were a number of applications that had been submitted and rejected and the design process took an entire decade to

LEFT The Circum-Baikal Road, the historical part of the Trans-Siberian Railway

complete. Some suggestions included using ferries rather than bridges for crossing rivers but the architects succeeded in having plans for a continuous railway agreed. Sergei Witte, the then finance minister was responsible for overseeing the building of the project while engineers began work on both ends of the line. By 1898 construction – undertaken by convicts and Russian

ABOVE The Glacier
Express crosses a
bridge in Switzerland

soldiers alike – had reached Lake Baikal (the largest, deepest and oldest lake in the world). The railway ended each side of the lake and an icebreaker ferry was bought to connect the two lines.

The coming of the railway gave Siberia a tremendous boost in agriculture enabling exports to central Russia and Europe. The Trans-Siberian Railway still remains a vital link in Russia's transportation services and around 30% of exports are still carried by train. Domestically it is also a crucial link for local passengers as well as the huge array of tourists from across the globe.

Glacier Express

TO TRAVEL FROM ZERMATT IN Switzerland to St Moritz on a seven and a half hour journey there is only one route to take and it's the Glacier Express. Alternatively passengers can take the train from Piz Bernina to the Matterhorn which crosses 291 bridges and steams through 91 tunnels before crossing the Oberalp Pass at more than 2,000 metres above sea level. This stunning panoramic journey through the Swiss Alps is simply breathtaking and passengers can enjoy views of central Switzerland, the Graubünden region, Lake Lucerne and Lucerne. The Glacier Express also passes through the Valais region with its glaciers and the mountain forests as well as meandering alongside Alpine meadows, mountain streams and valleys.

Those with the resources to travel on the Glacier Express were regular visitors in the 1920s who brought about the transformation of Zermatt and St Moritz from sleepy remote villages into up and coming resorts. During the 1920s, there were three railway companies in the region including VZ (later BVZ), RhB and FOB. All three railways realised the potential of the tourist industry and in 1926 the route between Valais and Graubünden was opened. Despite the relative advances of the day it was to take another 50 years before it was possible to travel through the Furka region during the cold winter months. In 1930 the Visp to Brig route was opened and the train made its inaugural journey between Zermatt and St Moritz.

Two companies VZ and RhB were equipped with electric engines however steam was the only mode of travel with FOB. The steam locomotives were eventually sent to Vietnam in the mid-1940s but returned home five decades later and have been providing today's passengers with nostalgic train rides since the early 1990s. Also during the 1940s, due to the unsettled environment as a result of World War II, services were scaled down and were only reintroduced in 1948 where changes were evident. The following two decades brought developments and faster engines were brought in to cut costs and bring down travelling times – as was happening across Europe, the UK and the US. It was during the 1970s that work was carried out on the Furka alpine route to ensure that the line was safe through the winter months. The route was finally ready for all-year travel in 1982.

The 1980s and 1990s proved to be a boom time for the Glacier Express and tourists flocked to ride on the famous train in their droves. In June 2005, the Glacier Express celebrated 75 years of service and is a tourist attraction that the Swiss are as proud of today as they were more than seven decades ago.

BELOW The Glacier Express going around a bend by a rocky stream in Switzerland

Flying Scotsman

BETWEEN LONDON'S King's Cross station and Edinburgh Waverley is 390 miles of East Coast Main Line that the Flying Scotsman, possibly one of the most famous steam trains in the world, used to regularly travel up and down. The line itself was built by three companies during the Victorian period with the first section between London and Doncaster having been constructed by Great Northern Railway. Work was finished in 1853, however, it took the North Eastern Railway another 23 years to build and finish the next stretch of line between Doncaster and Berwick.

The final section of the line was finished first by the North British Railway from Berwick to Edinburgh in 1846. A terminus was built at York within the city walls and trains, whether travelling north or south, were required to reverse into the original station. A new station alleviated the problem in 1877, however, trains were faced with the same issue at Newcastle station as the site in the city was also built as a terminus. The problem was solved with the King Edward VII Bridge built in 1906. The line remained pretty much as it was built originally except when a 13-mile diversion to avoid subsidence over an active mining area was constructed around Selby coalfield in 1983. Today the line is operated by Great North Eastern Railway (GNER).

Service began for this famous train in 1923. The official name of the flying Scotsman was the "Special Scotch Express" which ran exclusively for first and second class ticket holders at 10am each day. The journey was incredibly long at more than 10 hours although lunch was served in York and passengers had 30 minutes to stretch their legs. More than 25 years later, the Flying Scotsman became accessible to

the wider public when third class tickets were introduced in 1888. The train had rival companies wanting to offer a faster service than the infamous locomotive and the Flying Scotsman ended up reducing its journey time to eight and a half hours when it ran non-stop. After 1924, the train's name was changed from the Special Scotch Express and the Flying Scotsman was born, as was the non-stop service between London and Edinburgh in 1928.

In a response to the decline of steam, the train journey was again reduced between 1932 and 1938 but World War II brought changes and overcrowding was common. Despite the speed of the HSTs, the National Railway Museum was hoping to re-licence the Flying Scotsman during 2007 so that it would once more grace the East Coast Main Line.

LEFT The Flying Scotsman leaving King's Cross on a trip to Edinburgh, 1969

Chapter 9

The Demise of Steam

ALTHOUGH STEAM LOCOMO-TIVES did persevere in certain parts of the globe up until the end of the 20th century, their demise was in reality much earlier during the first part of the century when diesel and electric engines were developed and championed. Many steam trains did manage to hold on until around the mid-1900s, but for others, new trains meant new horizons and the age of steam was over.

Steam locomotives are quite simplistic mechanically and need constant maintenance with fairly primitive tools and working parts. They also require a great deal of fuel and on the whole they can be relatively inefficient. Labour is intensive and water is essential – both for the engine and the railwaymen! Steam trains need to be boiled up for a number of hours before they are

operational and at the end of each day all ash and clinker – industrial waste – need to be cleared and with the new developments in mechanical engineering the steam locomotive just wasn't a particularly viable option any more. In addition, the car was emerging as the new mode of transport and many influential politicians and businessmen alike were critical in seeing that road links were built and accessible for the masses.

By 1929, Denmark was the first country to champion the diesel engine. Many, built by Burmeister and Wain, had two bogies – a wheeled wagon – one of six wheels and the other on four. Frichs of Aarhus was another company making diesel engines that comprised a four-wheeled bogie, two driving axles and a trailing carrying axle. The main difficulty with diesel engine design at the beginning was transmission. By the 1960s, most of the UK, the rest of Europe and the US were all largely driven by diesel despite earlier teething problems. By the following decade, diesel locomotives swept the railways on a global scale and the change from steam to diesel was nothing if not rapid. Diesel was a cheaper, more efficient engine and was available and easily housed at night much more quickly than its pre-decessor. However, diesel engines were prone to breaking down.

In Ireland, despite never having had the same resources to coal and water as railways in many other countries and regions, the railway was to many a lifeline. While the railways of Northern Ireland were left by the government to fall apart, the Republican government did everything they could to keep the system going – even burning turf –

BELOW A derelict railway engine

before they too had to admit defeat and move with the times by employing diesel locomotives.

While across the water, English branch lines had long been suffering from underuse and by the 1950s the situation looked futile. Buses, if not more so than cars, were a real competitor and not only was this the cheapest mode of transport available, with countless bus stops, stations and numerous vehicles, buses also virtually dropped passengers at their own front doors. British Railways also gave up their lines for the novelty vehicle – the railbus.

By 1973 the Advanced Passenger Train or APT was beginning to come to prominence and by the middle of 1975 the High Speed Train, HST, was also making its debut. But despite advances in technology and easier, cheaper ways of doing things there is one man that ardent steam train enthusiasts hold responsible for the decline and subsequent disappearance of the steam locomotives. The name synonymous with their demise is Dr Richard Beeching.

The Labour Party's 1945 General Election manifesto promised to nationalise the nation's transport systems – except private cars and lorries operated

LEFT Rusting locomotives in a siding covered in graffiti referring to the cuts made in the Beeching report

by companies for their own business practices – which was carried out in the Transport Act of 1947. Under the British Transport Commission the remit was to run an integrated transport service that included the railways. In practice, integration was far from what was achieved and the 1951 Conservative government had very little to do to de-nationalise the roads. For years, road haulage companies had been able to undercut the railways who were tied to carrying goods at a fee set out by Parliament.

Then in 1960 an executive committee was formed, including Beeching, and the first report from the newly formed group was the recommendation to disband the British Transport Commission. Beeching became the chairman of British Railways and carried out various studies into the way the railways were run. Nicknamed the "Beeching Axe" due to its somewhat drastic and brutal recommendations, the report was reactionary to the significant losses suffered by the railways due to increased car power and the cheaper bus fares. Beeching, like many others, believed that the railways were the Victorian past and that although

the main lines could still prove to be profitable the lesser lines were more of a hindrance and a drain on resources than anything else. He certainly did not think that by closing stations and shutting down branch lines he was cutting òff the heartbeat of the nation – which many of his critics firmly believed he was doing.

However, the closures had already begun in the 1950s and in reality Beeching just stepped the pace up a gear and continued with the work that had already been implemented. Due to influential "voices" and some political manoeuvring not all lines destined to close were closed and some that were due to be kept operational closed in their place. Beeching's second report in 1964 was even more brutal and had the then Labour government not intervened the UK would surely have been left with a central but very short railway network of just 7,000 miles of track. Beeching resigned in 1965.

Chapter 10

Preserved Steam Railways Today

IT IS STILL POSSIBLE TO TRAVEL BY steam today thanks to an army of volunteers across the UK who refused to let the magic of steam die with the then government's plan to modernise the railways more than 50 years ago. From the old who remember the glory days, to the very young who want to ride on Thomas the Tank Engine, steam trains are still a popular pastime for many and preservation lines up and down the country continue to delight and thrill the passengers who travel on them.

The Railway Modernisation Plan of 1955 planned to phase out steam locomotives due to spiralling costs and significant losses endured by the railways. Dr Richard Beeching was commissioned

to write a report of recommendations The Re-shaping of British Railways which – to the horror of steam enthusiasts nationwide and those who relied on the railways – advocated the wholesale closure of "little-used" and "unprofitable" railway lines, the removal of stopping passenger trains and the closure of local stations on some lines.

The developments in road transport had led to huge losses on the railways and the government had to do something. But, despite the recommendations to develop certain aspects of the locomotives and their lines, the author of the report recommended that only drastic action would ensure that increasing losses didn't escalate any further. Successive governments were more interested in cost-saving rather than investing and more than 5,000 miles of railway lines (roughly a quarter) and 2,300 stations (nearly half) were closed. As part of an advisory committee, Beeching's thinking was that the railways should be run as a business not a public service. He strongly believed that if branch lines were unable to "pay their way" then they should be closed so that the core, more stable lines, would remain profitable.

A band of volunteers quickly began saving locomotives and rolling stock from breaker's yards with the help of finances gleaned from a wide variety of sources. Even today, preservation

BELOW The preserved train Bittern

lines rely heavily on the volunteers who willingly give up their time to maintain and preserve the engines, stock and lines which are expensive to run where costs are rising in specialised machinery and infrastructure. These passionate volunteers are crucial to the survival of preservation lines. Without them the history of what was arguably the UK's greatest technological gift to the world

will disappear forever.

Here are some of the journeys that can still be enjoyed today:

Bodmin & Wenford Railway – Cornwall

THE BODMIN & WENFORD RAILway begins at the modern Bodmin Parkway station some distance from the town itself and is the only preserved line that is served by High Speed Trains. The preserved line is around six and a half miles long and takes passengers over the River Fowey before embarking on a fairly steep climb along the Cornish countryside to the heights of Bodmin Moor. The outbound journey to Bodmin General Station takes around 25 minutes where passengers can alight and take a look around the two large locomotive sheds and station facilities before the quicker – it's downhill – return journey. The line was originally

LEFT A train on the Bodmin and Wenford line

opened by the Great Western Railway in 1887.

For details visit:
www.bodminandwenfordrailway.
co.uk

Paignton & Dartmouth Steam Railway – Devon

STARTING AT PAIGNTON STA-TION in the town centre, the line takes passengers along the cliffs overlook-ing Torbay before reaching its final destination beside the River Dart. The line was reopened – the same year it closed – by the Dart Valley Railway in 1972. The steam engines on the line are all GWR locomotives that origi-nally served the main line to London Paddington. The line today runs a num-ber of engines that were saved from the breaker's yard in Barry, South Wales. The start of the journey is a fairly steep ascent past Broadsands and Hookhills before descending to the River Dart. Passengers can alight and take the ferry across the harbour or stop and enjoy the picturesque market town of Dartmouth.

For details visit:
www.paignton-steamrailway.co.uk

South Devon Railway – Devon

THIS JOURNEY BEGINS AT BUCKFAST-leigh and takes passengers along the River Dart through the river valley to a quick stop at Staverton. From here the train travels to Totnes and the entire journey takes around 25 minutes.

The railway was preserved by a group of businessmen who decided that the line could be run as a commercial enterprise. The project failed but was taken up by a group of volunteers who today run the line as a registered charity. The views of the River Dart from this former Great Western Railway line are spectacular and the line relies heavily on passing tourists to keep it operational.

For details visit:
www.southdevonrailway.org

Swanage Railway – Dorset

SWANAGE STATION VERY NEARLY didn't become part of a preservation line when the local council acquired the site for redevelopment. However, the council asked for public opinion about reopening the station and the response was overwhelming. The line is a particularly picturesque route along the Purbeck line from Swanage through Corfe Castle to Norden and is used by locals that supported it as a mode of transport and not simply for recreational journeys. The former line served as a link to London Waterloo and the station and engines have been restored to their former 1930s glory. The six-mile journey takes around 25 minutes.

For details visit: www.swanagerailway.co.uk

West Somerset Railway – Somerset

FROM BISHOPS LYDEARD TO MINEhead, passengers can enjoy the longest preserved railway in the country which runs along the West Somerset Railway for 20 miles. When the line closed in 1971, the local council bought it and the route was re-established in 1976. The station at Bishops Lydeard has a visitor's centre, sheds, signal box and model railway. Passengers are taken via Crowcombe Heathfield on the initial leg of the journey to Stogumber. Williton station is halfway and passengers then enjoy sea views before descending into Watchet. The next stop is Washford followed by Blue Anchor before reaching Minehead. The railway was originally opened in 1862.

For details visit:
www.west-somerset-railway.co.uk

Bluebell Railway – East Sussex

THE BLUEBELL RAILWAY WAS RE-opened in 1960 and is one of the old-est preserved railways in the country. The line runs from Sheffield Park station near Brighton and carries passengers on a picturesque journey through the woods that are resplendent with bluebells in May, after which the line is named. The train then journeys to Horsted Keynes where the working sheds are located. Passengers then head

north to Sharpthorne Tunnel which is the longest tunnel on a preserved railway at 710 metres before reaching the station at Kingscote. The original line, opened in 1882, was part of the London Brighton and South Coast Railway.

For details visit:
www.bluebell-railway.co.uk

Mid-Hants Railway

FROM ALTON STATION IT TAKES passengers on the Mid-Hants Railway along the "Watercress line" to Alresford. Opened during the late 1970s, the line was carefully restored to preserve the feeling of a branch line. Stations along the route each represent a different era of history on the railway which was originally opened in 1865 to connect Alton with Winchester. Built to mainline standards due to the heavy locomotives that used the line when it was used as a temporary substitute for the main line, the Watercress line was so named after the line transported watercress grown in the River Arle from Alresford to Waterloo.

For details visit: www.watercressline.
co.uk

The Battlefield Line – Leicestershire

IN 1485, RICHARD III WAS DEFEATED and fatally wounded in the Battle of Bosworth. The line is named after this historic event and runs for around four and a half miles between Shackerstone Station, near Market Bosworth, to the actual battlefield itself. The main station has a visitor's centre and when passengers first board the train it takes them along the Ashby Canal which opened before the railway was built in 1804. The trail around the battlefield gives passengers the chance to learn about the day that Richard III died on 22 August in the 15th century and Henry VII became the first Tudor monarch to take the throne of England.

For details visit:
www.battlefield-line-railway.co.uk

Foxfield Steam Railway – Staffordshire

BELOW Signal box and crossing, Nene Valley

THE JOURNEY ON THE FOXFIELD Steam Railway is picturesque through woods and fields passing by the Staffordshire Moors in the distance on the five-mile round trip from Blythe Bridge. Originally built in 1893 to carry coal from Foxfield Colliery, the line includes a particularly steep gradient out of the colliery before making its return journey. Coal had been mined at the site from the

1600s but it was almost 200 years later before the railway arrived. Today the Foxfield Steam Railway maintains 28 steam, diesel and electric locomotives as well as coaches and freight vehicles.

For details visit: www.foxfieldrailway. co.uk

Midland Railway – Derbyshire

THE MIDLAND RAILWAY IS A WORKing line that runs between the stations of Butterley, Hammersmith, Riddings and Swanwick. Journeys generally begin at Butterley and head over the Butterley Reservoir on a large embankment that was built to replace the original bridge in the 1930s. The reservoir originally fed the Cromford Canal which was itself built to service the Grumblethorpe Colliery. Preservation work began under the direction of the Midland Railway Trust in 1973. There is also a country park for visitors to enjoy while the main site at Swanwick has a dedicated museum with a large collection of steam locomotives.

For details visit: www.midlandrailwaycentre.co.uk

Nene Valley Railway – Cambridgeshire

THE NENE VALLEY RAILWAY RUNS from Wansford through Ferry Meadows – a large country park with a miniature steam train – to Orton Mere and Peterborough. The line runs for seven and a half miles through the flat Cambridgeshire countryside. The original line opened in 1845 and the Nene Valley Railway today uses the eastern part of the former line. In 1972, after 127 years of history, British Rail closed the line. Between 1974 and 1977 the Nene Valley Railway worked hard to restore the line and it reopened on 1 June 1977.

For details visit: www.nvr.org.uk

North Norfolk Railway – Norfolk

BELOW The Welsh Highland Railway

KNOWN AS THE POPPY LINE, THE North Norfolk Railway involves a 25-minute journey from Sheringham to Holt where passengers can enjoy the sea views of what was once part of the Midland & Great Northern Railway as well as the wooded hills, Kelling Heath and Sheringham Park. The line that was opened in 1887 and built by William Marriott now offers visitors a museum of the railway's history along with carefully restored stations, a museum signal box and shops. While on board the train there is an activity carriage for younger passengers on the 10.5-mile journey.

For details visit: www.nnr.co.uk

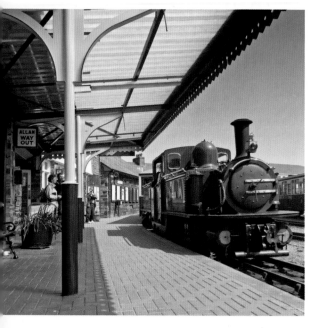

Brecon Mountain Railway – Wales

THE BRECON BEACONS ARE A POPular holiday destination for many in this idyllic part of Wales where the Brecon Mountain Railway is a narrow gauge railway. The journey begins at Pant which is situated to the north of Merthyr Tydfil in an area steeped in industrial invention history. Former quarries are visible which sourced the valuable limestone that was worked in the ironworks of Merthyr Tydfil. The three-mile journey finishes at Dol-y-Gaer having travelled through the Brecon Beacon National Park.

For details visit:
www.breconmountainrailway.co.uk

Welsh Highland Railway – Wales

THE WELSH HIGHLAND RAILWAY links Caernarfon in the north to Porthmadog in Cardigan Bay to the south. The journey takes passengers through the Snowdonia National Park on a narrow gauge railway. From Caernarfon the train climbs a steep hill which offers views of Yr Eifi and the mountains of Snowdonia. The journey passes through Dinas station – where the main workshops are located – before journeying through the Welsh countryside and the valley of the Afon Gwyrfai while enjoying views of the Cefn Du mountain. The train also passes close

to the base of Snowdon before the train begins its final leg of the journey towards Porthmadog.

For details visit: www.festrail.co.uk

North Yorkshire Moors Railway – Yorkshire

BEGINNING AT PICKERING, THE North Yorkshire Moors Railway line is a spectacular journey across the moors for 18 miles to Whitby. The station at Pickering has been restored to its former glory and also gives visitors the chance to view goods sheds and signal boxes. The journey takes around an hour and follows a route through the Newton Dale – an unspoiled valley that was cut by glacial activity during the last Ice Age. The train passes through Levisham Newtondale stations past Skelton Tower before climbing steeply up the valley. The journey reaches the summit of Fen Bog before arriving at Goathland. The railway maintains roughly

20 steam locomotives.
For details visit: www.nymr.co.uk

Dean Forest Railway – Gloucestershire

COAL AND IRON ORE HAVE TRA-DItionally been mined in the Forest of Dean since before Roman times but by

RIGHT Two trains passing each other in North Yorkshire

the late 1700s "railways" or wagon ways were being built to make transportation easier. These eventually became steam locomotive railways in some parts. The Dean Forest Railway began its life as a horse-drawn tram road in 1810 but was gradually converted to steam traction by the Severn & Wye Railway. Today, a four-mile stretch is operated by the Dean Forest Railway running from Lydney Junction to Norchard, Whitecroft and Parkend. The preservation of this railway was an arduous task as all the original buildings had disappeared. The railways engines were also in need of a great deal of work and had to be rescued from the breaker's yard at Barry in South Wales. The Dean Forest Railway is renowned for its special events on this historic line.

For details visit:
www.deanforestrailway.co.uk

East Somerset Railway – Somerset

ARTIST DAVID SHEPHERD IS THE

man responsible for the East Somerset Railway which he bought in 1967. The two-mile stretch has its main station at Cranmore which is the only remaining original station on the branch line. Passing through the Doulting Cutting – a Site of Special Scientific Interest – the train journey calls at Merryfield Lane (outbound) and Cranmore West (return) where there is the opportunity to view the replica of a Great Western Railway engine shed complete with workshops. One of the trains associated with the line is a rare Crane Tank which is originally from the steelworks in Staffordshire.

For details visit:
www.eastsomersetrailway.com

Gloucestershire and Warwickshire Railway – Gloucestershire

ALSO KNOWN AS GWR AND NOT to be mistaken for Great Western Railways, the Gloucestershire and Warwickshire Railway has 10 miles of line between Cheltenham and Broadway but is set to reach Stratford-upon-Avon at some point in its future. Preservation of this line has involved the building of platforms, buildings and artefacts and the careful repair and maintenance of locomotives and carriages. The station at Cheltenham racecourse was re-opened in 2003 and the GWR won the Ian Allan Independent Railway of the Year Award. The journey lasts around 90 minutes running south from Toddingham through the Vale of

LEFT A steam train at Grosmont station

Evesham and along the Cotswold escarpment before reaching the remains of Hailes Abbey. The train then wends its way to Didbrook and the Greet Tunnel – the second longest tunnel on a preserved railway at 633 metres – before skirting Dickston Hill, reaching Gotherinton Station and finally Cheltenham Racecourse.

For details visit: www.gwsr.com

Launceston Steam Railway – Cornwall

THE LAUNCESTON STEAM RAIL-

way re-opened in 1983 and is a two-mile stretch along the valley of the River Kensey. The journey also takes passengers through Hunts Crossing and then the train stops at New Mills which has a farm park. The line originally served the lines to London Waterloo and Exeter as well as branch lines to Wadebridge and Padstow – both in North Cornwall. When the line was excavated a 1,000 year old priory was rediscovered. Passengers can view these ruins as they travel on the narrow gauge railway.

For details visit:
www.launcestonsr.co.uk

Isle of Wight Steam Railway – Isle of Wight

THE ISLE OF WIGHT BECAME A popular holiday destination when Victorians followed in the footsteps of their monarch who regularly holidayed at

RIGHT The railway line leading out of Cranmore Station on the East Somerset Railway

Osborne House. It was around this time that the railway came to the island. Two lines are preserved today and are linked by an interchange station and the Ryde-Shanklin line – which is still part of the national railway system – is the best way to reach the Isle of Wight Steam Railway. The journey runs along railway tracks for around five miles on expertly restored rolling stock through Havenstreet and extremely picturesque woodlands that are abundant with bluebells during the spring. *For details visit: www.iwsteamrailway. co.uk*

Kent and East Sussex Railway – Kent and East Sussex

BUILT BY LIEUTENANT COLONEL Holman Frederick Stephens, the Kent and East Sussex Railway originally ran from Robertsbridge to Headcorn from

1903. The first section of the line re-opened in 1974 and there are around 10 miles of track between Tenterden and Bodiam which transports passengers to the magnificent 14th century castle which

LEFT A royal visitor on the Isle of Wight Steam Railway

is maintained by the National Trust. Some of the original station buildings survived and most passengers join the train at Tenterden where the station is an original.

For details visit: www.kesr.org.uk

Romney, Hythe and Dymchurch Railway – Kent

THIS MINIATURE RAILWAY WAS first opened in 1927 created by Captain Jack Howey who wanted to build a mainline railway in miniature with a double track, stations and powerful locomotives that were capable of speeds of up to 75mph. Howey originally ordered nine steam locomotives, five of which were based on Sir Nigel Gresley's Pacific design for LNER, two freight trains and two Canadian-style locomotives. It became the world's smallest public railway and flourished during the 1930s. It is still flourishing today and is especially popular with younger travellers.

For details visit: www.rhdr.org.uk

Bure Valley Railway – Norfolk

THE BURE VALLEY RAILWAY OPENED in 1990 and became the longest miniature railway to be built in the UK since the beginning of the 20th century. The journey stretches for nine miles and runs between Wroxham and Aylsham and is also a working line for local passengers as well as tourists. The 15-inch gauge railway is built on an original Great Eastern Railway branch line that linked Norwich and Cromer through the Norfolk countryside. The line was operational until 1980 and only remained closed for 10 years before the Bure Valley Railway took its place. The train passes Little Hautbois Hall before running parallel to the River Bure. The grave of Black Beauty author Anna Sewell can be found in the churchyard at St Andrew. The journey then travels past Buxton before finally reaching Aylsham station. Passengers may also enjoy walks along the Bure Valley along a vast network of routes.

For details visit: www.bvrw.co.uk

Great Central Railway – Leicestershire

ONCE PART OF THE GREAT CENtral Railway on the main line between Nottingham and Marylebone, today's Great Central Railway starts at Loughborough with the largest preserved railway station. The location is also the site of a number of work sheds and an engine shed, and incorporates the original signal box that still works and operates the train's movements. The station also encompasses a museum offering passengers a glimpse into the history of the railway which was originally intended by Sir Edward Watkin to become part of a continuous line from the north of the UK under the English Channel to France.

For details visit: www.gcrailway.co.uk

LEFT Loughborough sheds

The pictures in this book were provided courtesy of the following:

GETTY IMAGES
101 BAYHAM STREET, LONDON NW1 0AG

MR DAVID COOPER

Cover Design & Updates: ALEX YOUNG

Image research by: ELLIE CHARLESTON

Published under licence from: G2 ENTERTAINMENT LTD

Publisher: JULES GAMMOND

Written by: CHARLIE MORGAN